OBEYD-E ZAKANI

Ethics of The Aristocrats
&
Other Satirical Works

Edited and Translated from the Persian
with an Introduction and Notes by

HASAN JAVADI

Including
Cat & Mouse
Translated by Dick Davis

MAGE PUBLISHERS

First edition published by Jahan Books Co. in 1985 as
'Obeyd-e Zakani:
The Ethics of the Aristocrats and other Satirical Works.

The cover photo, courtesy of the Fog Art Museum, is a seventeenth-century Indian painting for *Ta'rifat-e Mulla Dopiazeh,* a Safavid work that was a copy of Obeyd-e Zakani's *Ta'rifat* (Definitions).

Library of Congress Cataloging-in-Publication Data
'Ubayd Zakani, Nizam al-Din, d. ca. 1370.
[Poems. English. Selections]
Obeyd-e Zakani, ethics of the aristocrats & other satirical
works / edited and translated from the Persian with
an introduction and notes by Hasan Javadi. -- Paberback ed.
p. cm.
"Cat & Mouse Translated by Dick Davis."
Includes bibliographical references and index.
ISBN 1-933823-22-4 (pbk. : alk. paper)
I. Javadi, Hasan. II. Davis, Dick. III. Title.
PK6550.U2A2 2008
891'.5511--dc22
2007046994
Second soft cover edition
ISBN 1-933823-22-4
ISBN 13: 978-1-933823-22-5

Printed and manufactured in U.S.A.

MAGE BOOKS ARE AVAILABLE AT BOOKSTORES,
THROUGH THE INTERNET
OR DIRECTLY FROM THE PUBLISHER:
MAGE PUBLISHERS, 1032-29TH STREET NW
WASHINGTON, DC 20007
202-342-1642 • AS@MAGE.COM • 800-962-0922
VISIT MAGE ONLINE AT
WWW.MAGE.COM

CONTENTS

INTRODUCTION

Nezam al-Din Obeyd-e Zakani was one of the most remarkable poets, satirists and social critics of Iran, but his works have not received proper attention. Often dismissed by conservative scholars as a writer of bawdy stories and obscene verses, it is only in the last few decades that his work has received serious consideration.

The details of Obeyd's life are scant at best. It is believed that he was born in Qazvin around the year 1300, and that his family was originally from an Arab tribe called Zakanian which, after coming to Iran, settled in a village near Qazvin. A contemporary of Obeyd, the historian Hamd Allah Mostofi, refers to him with great respect as "the exalted master Nezam al-Din Obeyd Ullah Zakani," and refers to his "excellent poems and matchless works of prose." Mostofi adds that the poet was descended from Arabs of the Banu Khafaja tribe that had settled in Qazvin long before his time. Also, according to the same source, the family members were notable in two areas: theology and government service. Mostofi's *Tarikh-i Guzida*, which provides us with this information, was written around the year 1330. Since Obeyd was well known and respected at this date, his twentieth century editor, Abbas Iqbal, deduces that he must have been born around the turn of the fourteenth century.[1] At the library of Haj Husayn Agha Malek in Tehran, there is a manuscript copy of *Asmar va Ashjar* by Ali Shah bin Mohammad bin Ghassem Kharazmi, known as Ala' Bokhari, the Astronomer, in the handwriting of Obeyd. On the second page of this manuscript, Obeyd gives 11 Muharram 768 (September 17, 1366) as the date he finished

---

1 Hamd Allah Mostofi, *Tarikh-i Guzida*, ed. A.H. Nawa'i, Tehran, 1957, pp. 845–46.

copying it. It was on this date that Isfahan was conquered by Shah Shoja. Obeyd's son, Ishaq, has written the following in the margin of the manuscript: "Passed down to me by the right of inheritance in the year 772." From this one can deduce that Obeyd passed away in Isfahan on or before the year 772 (1370).

Due to his title, "the exalted master," some scholars suggest that Obeyd held a high official position, but there is no evidence to support this claim. In a poem addressed to his patron, Shah Shoja, Obeyd writes:

I have always been endeared by kings;
From the time of youth until this day and age. [2]

Obeyd, however, was not "endeared" by Shah Shoja's father, whom he had been forced to flee. After wandering through various cities for several years, Obeyd joined the court of Shah Shoja. A story, in the *Tazkirat ul-Shu'ara* ("Biographies of the Poets") of Dawlatshah (1487) also casts doubt on Obeyd's statement about his life-long endearment by kings. Dawlatshah writes:

It has been related that he [Obeyd] had composed a treatise on Rhetoric in the name of Shah Abu Ishaq that he desired to present to the king. But he was told that the king was busy with his jester (and had no time for him). Obeyd was astonished and wondered: 'If the king's most intimate society could be accessible through jesting and ribaldry and the jesters become his favorites and courtiers, whereas the men of accomplishment and learning be deprived of his favors, why should one trouble himself and bother his brain with the smoke of the lamp of the school?' Without attaining an audience with the king, he returned and wrote this wonderful quatrain:

In the arts and learning be not proficient like me,
Lest by the great you will be despised like me.
If you desire favors from the masters of our time
Beg shamelessly, play the lute and be a libertine.

---

2 See Ardashir Bahmani, "Obeyd Shaer-i hazl va hajv", *Armaghan*, vol. 45, Nos. 7–8, 1971, p. 434.

A friend criticized him, saying: 'In spite of your accomplishments and talents, to abandon learning and virtue in favor of ribaldry and lewd utterances does not seem logical.' Obeyd recited this poem for him:

> *Keep clear of learning, sir, if so you may,*
> *Lest you should lose your pittance for the day.*
> *Play buffoon and learn the fiddler's skill:*
> *On great and small you may then work your will!*[3]

Although this might have been a very true picture of the age of Obeyd, it does not seem to be historically in tune with the other facts of his life. Of course the possibility of such an incident cannot be ruled out entirely. However, since we know that Obeyd came from Qazvin to the court of Shiraz during the reign of Shah Abu Ishaq, at a time when he was well-known, it is safe to assume that such treatment would not have been accorded him, even if he did not have any official position.

The history of Iran in the fourteenth century consists of a succession of wars and disruptions resulting in the rise and fall of numerous regional dynasties. In 1256 Hulagu, a grandson of the great Mongol conqueror Chengiz Khan, had led his expedition to the west and destroyed the Isma'ili strongholds in the Alborz mountains. Two years later, he had brought to an end more than five hundred years of rule by the Abbasid caliphs in Baghdad. The Il-Khanid dynasty, founded by Hulagu, lasted until 1335. Although its history is accompanied by considerable bloodshed and atrocities, some of its kings, such as Ghazan Khan (1295–1304) and his brother Uljaitu (1305–1316), became patrons of literature and culture. Their capitals, Tabriz and Sultanieh, were prosperous metropolises where envoys and merchants from the East and West met. Obeyd's early life must have coincided with the reign of Abu Sa'id Bahador Khan (1316–1335), upon whose death the Il-Khanid empire became a bone of contention between various Mongol princes. It was not until the rise of another bloodthirsty Tartar conqueror, Tamerlane,

---

3 *Kulliyat-e Obey-e Zakani*, Tehran, 1953, p. 73.

that their fighting came to an end (between 1360 and 1387), as did the rule of many other princes.

Of the dynasties that ruled over Iran and were more or less contemporary with Obeyd, the Houses of Inju and Muzaffar should be mentioned here, as the life and fortunes of our poet were related to them. Of these two dynasties an interesting account is given by Gertrude Bell in the introduction to her *Poems from the Divan of Hafiz* (William Heinemann, 1928):

About the time of the birth of Hafiz, that is to say in the beginning of the fourteenth century, a certain Mahmud Shah Inju was governing the province of Fars, of which Shiraz is a capital, in the name of Abu Sa'id.... On the death of Mahmud Shah, Abu Sa'id appointed Sheikh Hussein ibn Chuban to the governorship of Fars, a lucrative and much-coveted post. Sheikh Hussein took the precaution of ordering the three sons of Mahmud Shah to be seized and imprisoned; but while they were passing through the streets of Shiraz in the hands of their captors, their mother who accompanied them, lifted her veil and made a touching appeal to the people, calling upon them to remember the benefits they had received from their late ruler. Her words took instant effect; the inhabitants rose, released her and her sons, and drove Sheikh Hussein into exile. He, however returned with an army supplied by Abu Sa'id, and induced Shiraz to submit to his rule. In 1335, a year or two after these events, Abu Sa'id died, and the power of the house of Hulagu crumbled away. There followed a long period of anarchy, which was brought to an end when Uwais, another descendant of Hulagu, seized the throne. He and his son Ahmad reigned in Baghdad until Ahmad was driven out by the invading army of Timur. But during the years of anarchy the authority of the Sultan of Baghdad had been considerably curtailed. On Abu Sa'id's death, Abu Ishaq, one of the three sons of Mahmud Shah Inju who had so narrowly escaped from the hands of Sheikh Hussein, took possession of Shiraz and Isfahan, finally ousting his old enemy, while Mohammad ibn Muzzafer, who had earned a name for valor in the service of Ibu Sa'id, made himself master of Yezd....[4]

Abu Ishaq had not steered his bark into quiet waters. In 1340 Shiraz was besieged and taken by a rival Atabeg, and the son of Mahmud Shah was obliged to content himself with Isfahan. But in the following year he returned, captured Shiraz by a stratagem, and again established himself ruler over all Fars. The remaining years of his reign are chiefly occupied with military expeditions against Yezd, where Mohammad ibn Muzaffar and his sons were building up a formidable power. In 1352, determined to put an end to these attacks, Mohammad marched into Fars and laid siege to Shiraz. Abu Ishaq, whose life was one of perpetual dissipation, redoubled his orgies in the face of danger. Uncertain of the fidelity of the people of Shiraz, he put to death all the inhabitants of two quarters of the town, and contemplated insuring himself of a third quarter in a similar manner. But these measures did not lead to the desired results. The chief of the threatened quarter got wind of the king's design, and delivered up the keys of his gate to Shah Shuja', the son of Mohammad ibn Muzaffar, and Abu Ishaq was obliged to seek refuge a second time in Isfahan. Four years later, in 1357, he was given up to Mohammad, who sent him to Shiraz and, with a fine sense of dramatic fitness, had him beheaded before the ruins of Persepolis.[5]

The last forty years of Obeyd's life coincided with the reigns of Abu Ishaq, Mubarez al-Din Mohammad (1313–1357) and his son Shah Shoja (1357–1384). Obeyd often dedicated his non-satirical works to his contemporary kings or their ministers. Although the number of such works by Obeyd is small, a few of his poems shed some light on his life.

One of his earliest works, entitled *Nawadir al-Amthal* (Chosen Proverbs), is a collection of wise sayings and proverbs in Arabic and is dedicated to Khajeh Ala al-Din Mohammad. He was a native of Farimad in Khorasan and a protégé of the well-known minister and

---

4 Dawlatshah Samarqandi, *Tazkirat ul-Shu'ara*, Tehran, 1958, p. 324; and E. G. Browne, *A Literary History of Persia under Tartar Dominion*, Cambridge, 1920, III, pp. 232–33.

5 Gertrude Bell, *Poems from the Divan of Hafez*, London, 1928, pp. 8–11.

historian Rashid al-Din Fazl Allah. Ala al-Din became the minister of Abu Sa'id for only six months in 1321 and then assumed another post in Khorasan, where he was killed in 1336. Since Obeyd apparently never went to Khorasan, the book must have been dedicated in the year 1321. This could account for the fact that, according to Hamd Allah Mostofi, Obeyd was known as an author and scholar in 1330. Another minister to whom Obeyd dedicated a number of his poems is Rukn al-Din Amid al-Mulk, Abu Ishaq's minister in 1346. Obeyd in one poem addressed to this minister says: "It is now twelve years since my fortunate star brought me to your palace." In another poem he sets the date of his coming from his native Qazvin to Shiraz at ten years earlier, so this must have been in the years 1334–46.

Chronologically the first king to whom Obeyd dedicated any of his works was Abu Ishaq, who was also the patron and friend of the great poet Hafez (1326–1389). Apart from a number of panegyrics addressed to Abu Ishaq, Obeyd dedicated his 'Ushshaq-Nameh (Book of lovers) to him in 1350. The work evidently is written in emulation of a *mathnavi* by Iraqi (1211–1289) with the same name. It is a love story in some 750 couplets in the form of a *mathnavi* interspersed with occasional *ghazals*. Whereas the poem of Iraqi celebrates mystical love, Obeyd's poem presents love in a more sensual manner.

Abu Ishaq, because of his taste for poetry and learning as well as his generosity, had attracted a brilliant circle of poets and scholars. Several of Obeyd's poems celebrate the reign of Abu Ishaq and describe Shiraz as the center of culture and learning. In two poems he refers to a famous palace whose construction began by the order of Abu Ishaq in 1353 in Shiraz. The Arab traveler Ibn Battuta, who visited Shiraz between the years 1340 and 1350, related that during the construction of this palace the inhabitants of the city vied with each other to participate in the construction; men of all ranks came out to do the work, putting on their best clothes and digging the foundations with silver spades.[6] Before the palace, which was

---

6 Ibn Battuta, *Travels* quoted by A. J. Arberry in *Shiraz: Persian City of Saints and Poets*, University of Oklahoma Press, 1960, p. 53.

supposed to compete with the renowned Taq-i Kesra in Ctesiphon, could be completed, Abu Ishaq's life came to a sudden and tragic end. Obeyd in another poem, after describing the magnificent court of his patron, writes:

> *But look what a game the world did play with him,*
> *And how calamity took the reins of his happiness.*
> *The sea of misfortune surged suddenly forth,*
> *Engulfing his kingdom, his treasure and his son.*
> *Or perhaps the tears and pain, the fire of sighs*
> *That palace had caused, enkindled the great house...*
> *That garden of pleasure whose fragrance and hue*
> *Inspired the sacred gardens of heaven now is such*
> *That the nightingale no longer graces its perch,*
> *For the black-hearted crow there has made his nest.*
> *The palace from whose prosperity Fortune itself sought a share,*
> *Became a nest for the owl and a breeding place for dogs.*
> *Obeyd, of the works of time and the transience of the world*
> *A thousand hints can be gleaned.*[7]

The reign of Mubarez al-Din Mohammad did not last very long after the death of his rival Abu Ishaq. Mohammad was such a piti-less and harsh man that his own son, Shah Shoja, blinded him in 1358 and imprisoned him in Qa'la-ye Sefid in Fars; a few years later he died in Bam, near Kerman. Mubarez al-Din has been described as "brave and devout, but at the same time cruel, bloodthirsty, and treacherous."[8] It has been reported that Shah Shoja once asked him if he had killed a thousand men with his own hands. Mubarez al-Din thought for a while and said: "Just over eight hundred, to be exact."[9] On another occasion, two prisoners were brought to Mubarez al-Din while he was saying his prayers. Between two prayers, he took his sword, cut off their heads, and returned to his devotions undis-

---

7 *Kulliyat-e Obeyd*, pp. 67–69, and 81–82.

8 A. J. Arberry, *Classical Persian Literature*, London, 1958, p. 297.

9 Khandamir, *Habib al-Siyar*, III, p. 275.

turbed.[10] This particular incident very much resembles a passage in Obeyd's *Mush u Gorbeh* (The Mouse and the Cat; translated as *Rats Against Cats* by Masoud Farzad [Priory Press, 1945]) where the cat kills and eats a mouse and then goes to the mosque and devoutly performs his prayers. Obeyd was not alone in writing against Mubarez al-Din Mohammad's religious hypocrisy. The scholars of Shiraz nicknamed him Muhtasib" (Chief of Police)when he closed the taverns and forbade the drinking of wine. Hafez refers to those days of oppressive restrictions in one of his *ghazals*:

> *Though wine gives delight and the wind distills the perfume
>   of the rose,*
>
> *Drink not wine to the strains of the harp, for the constable
>   [muhtasib] is alert.*
>
> *Hide the goblet in the sleeve of the patch-work cloak,*
>
> *For the time, like the eye of the decanter, pours forth blood.*
>
> *Wash the wine-stain from your dervish-cloak with tears,*
>
> *For it is the season of piety and the time of abstinence.*"[11]

Looking with nostalgia to the by-gone years, Hafez, in another poem hopes that piety will not become synonymous with hypocrisy:

> *They have closed the doors of the wine-taverns;*
> *   O God, suffer not*
>
> *That they should open the doors of the house of deceit*
> *   and hypocrisy!*
>
> *If they have closed them for the sake of the heart of the*
> *   self-righteous zealot,*
>
> *Be of good heart, for they will reopen them for God's sake!*[12]

---

10 Ibid.

11 Browne, op. cit., p. 277.

12 Ibid, p. 278.The fanaticism of Mubarez al-Din Mohammad knew no bounds. It has been reported that around the year 1360–61 when he was the ruler of Bam and Kerman, as well as Isfahan and Yazd, in order "to strengthen the hand of the faith" in less than two years, he gathered four thousand manuscripts on philosophy and ordered them to be washed away. See further M. E. Bastani Parizi, *Asia-ye Haft Sang*, Tehran, 1967, p. 239.

Obeyd more than Hafez could not tolerate the rule of Mubarez al-Din and in 1357 fled Shiraz and went to the court of Sultan Uwais Ilkani (1337–1374). In a beautiful *ghazal,* Obeyd describes his plight and says that though his "heart bleeds" for leaving his beloved city, being "in danger" leaves him no other choice.[13] Apparently because of his liberal views, he was afraid of being accused of heresy. For five years Obeyd stayed in Baghdad. Shah Shoja, who had succeeded his father, was tricked and ousted from Shiraz by his brother Mahmud. Shah Shoja went to Kerman and ruled that province for some years until in 1365 he managed to take back Shiraz. Mahmud took refuge in Isfahan and once with the help of Sultan Uwais's troops fought with Shah Shoja, but neither side had any victory. It was in 137. that both Mahmud and Sultan Uwais died, then Shah Shoja not only occupied Isfahan but also held sway from Tabriz to Baghdad, and for a while became the master of the greater part of Iran. It seems that about the years 1362–63 Obeyd decided to return to Shiraz, but not liking Mahmud he went to the court of Shah Shoja in Kerman, and two years later accompanied him to his beloved city Shiraz.

At the court of Baghdad Obeyd met Salman-i Sawaji, who was the poet laureate of Sultan Uwais. Before their meeting their relationship was anything but cordial. Salman in a quatrain had called him a "cursed satirist," noted for his "obnoxiousness and heresy," who "is in truth only an ignorant country oaf from Qazvin."[14] Hearing this, Obeyd set off for Baghdad.

Here is the rest of this story in a translation by E. G. Browne:

> "On his arrival there, he found Salmán, surrounded with great pomp and circumstance, on the banks of the Tigris, occupied with pleasure and diversion and the society of the learned and accomplished men. When by some means he succeeded in entering the circle, Salman had just composed this hemistich descriptive of the Tigris, which he asked the bystanders to complete:

> *"'With drunken frenzy and fury fierce this year the Tigris flows'*

---

13 *Kulliyat-e Obeyd*, p.126; cf. pp.123, 111, and 129.

14 Dawlatshah Samarqandi, *Tazkirat ul-Shu'ara*, Tehran, 1958, p. 324; and Browne, op. cit., p. 223.

"Thereupon 'Ubayd-i-Zákání extemporized the following complimentary hemistich:

"'With its foaming lips and its feet in chains, 'twere mad,
you might suppose.'

"Salmán was delighted and inquired whence he came. He replied, 'From Qazvin.' In the course of the ensuing conversation Salmán asked him whether his name was known or any of his verse familiar in Qazvin, or not. 'Ubayd-i-Zákání replied, 'The following fragment of his poetry is very well-known:

"A frequenter of taverns am I, and a lover of wine,
Besotted with drink and desire at the Magians' shrine.
Like a wine-jar from shoulder to shoulder amongst them I pass,
And go from one hand to another like goblet or glass.'"

"'Now although Salmán is an accomplished man,' added 'Ubayd, 'and these verses may perhaps be truly ascribed to him, yet in my opinion they were most probably composed by his wife.'

"Salmán perceived from this witty speech that this was no one other than 'Ubayd himself, whereupon he made much of him, apologized for his satire, and so long as 'Ubayd remained in Baghdad, fell short in no service which he could render him. And 'Ubayd used often to say to him, 'O Salmán, fortune favored you in that you so speedily made your peace with me, and so escaped from the malice of my tongue!'"[15]

This story of Dawlatshah, as quoted here by Browne, seems to be a fabrication, because the poem extemporaneously completed by Obeyd is to be found in the recently published *Divan* of Naser Bokharai, a fourteenth century poet.(See Parviz Natel Khanlari in *Sokhan*, vol. 4, no. 6 [1953]. However, the story reflects the manner in which Obeyd was regarded as a wit and sharp-tongued satirist with access to leading figures of his day.

---

15 Browne, op. cit., pp. 234–35.

With the rule of Shah Shoja, the oppressive restrictions that had been imposed by his father were relaxed. The taverns were reopened and the sound of music could be heard again. Hafez says:

> *The harp began to clamor 'Where is the objector?'*
> *The cup began to laugh 'Where is the forbidder?'*[16]

In another poem he further celebrates the return of his patron to Shiraz:

> *At early dawn good tidings reached my ear from the Unseen*
> *Voice:*
> *'It is the era of Shah Shoja: drink wine boldly!'*
> *That time is gone when men of insight went apart*
> *With a thousand words in the mouth but their lips silent.*[17]

Obeyd himself voices his own happiness with the reign of Shah Shoja and in a long panegyric to him says:

> *Obeyd will not bewail the injustices of this time*
> *As good fortune threw him to this auspicious threshold.*
> *He was engulfed in the surging sea of sorrow,*
> *But your favors cast him on the shore of security.*[18]

Obeyd was with Shah Shoja when the latter conquered Isfahan in 1366, and in a poem he congratulated him on his victory. In another poem, dedicated to Shah Shoja, a few years later in 1370, Obeyd talks of his old age and the heartwarming patronage of the king. The year of his death has been given as 1370 or 1371. It is certain that in 1371 Obeyd was not alive, for his son, at the back of a book that had been transcribed by the poet, states that it had passed to him from his father by the right of inheritance.[19]

Turning to the social conditions of the period in which Obeyd lived, one finds it to be an age of moral depravity and social degradation. Some historians consider the Mongol invasion with its

---

16 Ibid, pp. 279–80.

17 Ibid, p. 279.

18 *Kulliyat-e Obeyd*, p. 42.

19 Ibid, introduction of Iqbal, p. 25.

incredible bloodshed and destruction the major cause of this
decline. Of course there is no denying that this was one of the
major factors, but the absence of a stable government for a rela-
tively long period of time and continued fighting among various
local emirs who took possession of one or more provinces of the
country created a chaotic situation in which no one was safe from
rapid changes of fortune. In 1295, Ghazan Khan converted to
Islam and until the death of Abu Sa'id in 1335 some measure of
normalcy returned, though occasional atrocities were commit-
ted by the Mongol emirs. The collapse of Il-Khanid rule ushered
in a period of bloodshed, murder, and court intrigues that are
very graphically depicted by Obeyd in his *Ethics of the Aristocrats*.
"These great and sagacious men whose existence honors the face of
the earth" – as Obeyd mockingly calls them – "believe neither in
the human soul nor in the world hereafter." Interestingly enough
Obeyd quotes even the verses of the Qur'an out of context in order
to demonstrate their points of view. For them "the supposed joys
of heaven and the sufferings of hell exist in this world. It is because
of this belief that for the life, the property, and the honor of the
people they have not the least consideration." For them "a cup of
fire-colored wine/is dearer than the blood of one hundred broth-
ers." Obeyd continues to describe in his piquant humor the beliefs
and manners of the aristocracy of his time, and very often what
he says is hardly an overstatement. He gives a vivid picture of the
moral degradation of the age, which is reminiscent of the *Satires* of
Juvenal at the time of Rome's decadence. Abbas Iqbal, the historian
of the Mongol period and Obeyd's editor, writes of this age:

> "The mother of one of the kings was known for prostitu-
> tion and promiscuity; the wife of another killed her husband
> in the most hideous way in bed, since he had imprisoned
> her lover; another wife in the hope of getting married to her
> brother-in-law urged him to depose his brother; another
> king blinded his father with his own hands and committed
> adultery with his mother; and a fourth monarch forced his

emirs to divorce their wives so that he could woo them and write love songs for them."[20]

Therefore, it is no wonder that Obeyd in his "Definitions" thus describes the ruling class of his time:

Nothing: *Their existence.*

Hollow: *Their civility.*

Vanity and Folly: *Their talk.*

Disapproval, Greed, Malice and Envy: *Their characteristics.*

The Anqa (phoenix) of the West: *Justice and Humanity.*

Roguery, Violence, Hypocrisy,
  Dissimulation and Falsehood: *The ways of the great men.*

Lust: *their ailment.*

Perhaps more than anyone else in Persian literature, Obeyd in his satirical works uniquely illustrates the social conditions of this period. It is true that some other poets such as Saif-i Farghani (d. circa 1347) and Awhadi of Maragha (1270–1337/8) vehemently attacked corruption and social injustices in their poems, but the wit and insight of Obeyd give his works a special character. Obeyd looks upon this world of extravagant indulgence and corruption with the censorious eye of a Juvenal and portrays it with the cynicism and wit of a Voltaire and the hilarious grotesqueness of a Rabelais. But underneath his cheerful irreverence and nonchalance there lie sorrow and bitterness. Seeing this scene of deceit, greed, lust, syco- phancy, perversion, scorn of the old values and virtues, extremes of wealth and poverty, violence, and bloodshed, he expresses his indig- nation in the form of scathing stories and sardonic maxims. He says: "Engage in ribaldry, cuckoldry, gossip, ingratitude, false testimony, selling heaven for the world, and playing the tambourine, so that you may become dear to the great and enjoy your life."

Though Obeyd expresses his religious sentiments and devotion in several of his poems, he has no time for the men who use religion in order to reach their worldly aims. With grinning irreverence he

---

20 Ibid, pp. 37–8.

dismisses the claims to piety of sheikhs and preachers. He says: "Don't believe the sermons of the clerics, lest you go astray and end up in hell." For him a Haji is a person who goes on pilgrimage to Mecca once and for the rest of his life swears falsely by the Ka'ba. In his "Definitions" a Sufi is called a "freeloader," and Obeyd has nothing but scorn for the hypocritical Sufis of his time. A Sufi is asked by a man if he wants to sell his patchwork cloak. A bystander says: "If a fisherman sells his net, how is he going to fish?" In two letters, which are full of obscure and ridiculous terminology, Obeyd lampoons the high flown esoteric style of the Sufis, their claims of communion with the Divine, and their state of spiritual expansion and contraction.

By contrast with ostentatious and sham-pious clerics and Sufis, Obeyd favors the true mystics whom he calls *rends* and *qalandars*. He says: "If you want salvation, attach yourself to the service of the all-sacrificing and pure-hearted *rends* in order to be saved." As is explained in the notes to this volume, a *qalandar* has similarities to the Malamatiyya dervishes, who were somewhat like the modern hippies on account of their unconventional dress, behavior, and way of life. They only performed very essential prayers and acts of devotion and laid a great emphasis on "purity of heart" rather than pretentious acts of piety and excessive asceticism. The difference between a Malamati and a *qalandar* is that while the former keeps his acts of devotion secret and even goes to the extent of pretending to be impious, the latter does not care for his outward appearance, nor does he conform with popular beliefs and manners only because everyone follows them. *Rend* is also a very difficult term to translate. Originally it meant something like a "rogue," but gradually it came to mean a "liberal-minded man," a "lover of truth," a "social rebel," or a "true Sufi." *Rend* in the poetry of Hafez has special significance. It stands for all the high and humane ideals that he talks about in his *Divan*. In short, it sometimes comes to mean the "perfect man."

Obeyd in a poem defines a "true Sufi" as "one who with pure wine has a pure heart." In another *ghazal* he describes himself as one "of a band of *qalandars*," withdrawn from the world and their hearts set on poverty, "in whose purse or hand there is no one's golden coin, nor in their hearts is there the sign of any coinage." Free from any writ, even free from the fear of non-existence, they are "the sultans of their time, though they have neither drums nor flags, [and]... under any circumstances they are reluctant to harm anyone." Then Obeyd asks: "Is it right to harm them?"[21] Obeyd seems to present himself not so much as a "true Sufi" or a *qalandar* as to use these terms to criticize the men of the cloak whom he describes with their rosaries as "asses, bells hanging from their necks." He advises, "Make yourself free from their hypocrisy and deceit. Sit with the fair and drink wine." While not being a practicing dervish of the Qalanda-riyya order, Obeyd favored their tenets and contrasted their idea of the "purity of the heart" and their candor with the hypocrisy and corruption of the people of his time.

While Obeyd is most known for his satire, he did produce a number of non-satirical works, which reflect his great poetic talent. This is especially true of his *ghazals*, which are both charming and beautiful and present an interesting contrast with his satirical works. A. J. Arberry notes in his *Classical Persian Literature*:

These poems deserve study not only for their own sake, but because they reveal their author as bridging the gap between Sa'dí and Háfiz, and introducing into the *ghazal* innovations that must assuredly have exercised influence on his junior contemporary who attended the same court circles.

Of "Ethics of the Aristocrats," written in 1340, some account was given earlier but a few more words should be added here. It is quite obvious that the title was inspired by a work of the great philosopher and statesman Nasir al-Din Tusi (1210–1274) entitled *Awsaf al-Ashraf* (Description of the Aristocrats). This latter work, which describes the Sufis, also could be titled "Characteristics of the Chosen Ones." Although the title given by Obeyd is very similar to this one, it is the famous *Akhlaq-i Naseri* ("Nasirian Ethics" by the same author), as well as other books on ethics with their high flown and pompous style, that Obeyd is parodying. He mockingly agrees with the great men of his age who have rejected the manners and beliefs of the past and started new ones. He writes, "As the nature of our

---

21 Ibid, p 92.

great men has been refined ... they have concentrated their undivided attention on the affairs of this world as well as the next, and in the eye of their judgment the customs and practices of the ancients seemed unfounded and contemptible." This is why Obeyd subdivides the chapters of his book into "The Abrogated Practice" and "The Adopted Practice." The former deals with traditional views on subjects such as justice, virtue, generosity, and the like, which every book on ethics highly recommends. The latter is Obeyd's satirical addition, and it sets forth the practices and beliefs of the ruling class of the time, which are of course exactly the opposite of the "abrogated" ideas. They believe that "justice bequeaths misfortune," and chastity, fidelity, generosity and courage are frowned upon as the characteristics of naïve and foolish men who don't know how to enjoy their lives. Obeyd concludes that he has written this "short treatise on the ethical principles of the ancients, now called "abrogated," as well as some accounts of the practices and character of the great men of our time, now considered "adopted," for the benefit of the students of this science and the novices of this path!"

As in most of his works the moral laxity of the gentry of his time is a special butt of satire for Obeyd. In the third chapter of "Ethics of the Aristocrats", he engages two celebrated heroes of the *Shahnameh* (Rostam and Houman) in a friendly homosexual contest. As Obeyd imitates and then parodies the language of Ferdowsi, it is hard to translate and imitate his style. Nevertheless, the chapter has been rendered into English here.

In the treatise entitled "One Hundred Maxims," Obeyd satirically treats the practice of writing "Books of Councils" which was done ad nauseam. By stating that he follows the example of Plato's maxims to Aristotle (as reported by Nasir al-Din Tusi) or those of Anushiravan to his vizier, Obeyd assumes an air of dignity, which before long is broken by his sarcastic pieces of advice. He ridicules the monitors of public morality by parodying their self-evident statements with his own, such as "Do not waste your time," "Do not spoil a good day" or "At any rate, avoid death because it has been disliked since the days of old." Then suddenly he takes up subjects that are shocking and sometimes obscene. "Sow your seeds unlawfully so that your children will become theologians, sheikhs and favorites of the king," or "As far as possible refrain from speaking the truth, so that you may not become a bore to other people, and so that they may not be annoyed by you for no obvious reason." At the end, Obeyd with his usual humor adds, "These are sayings that have reached us from our masters and from great men. Being a good Muslim, and out of kindness, we have related them here briefly so that the fortunate will practice them accordingly and benefit there from, and remember us in their prayers."

In his "Definitions," Obeyd finds another ingenious way to satirize the vices of society. In this brief and poignant satirical work, which resembles The *Devil's Dictionary* of Ambrose Bierce, Obeyd gives under ten different headings a cross section of different people and professions and his views on them. It is the epigrammatic quality and sharp sarcasm of the "Definitions" that makes them so memorable. He describes "The Judge" as "he who is cursed by everyone"; "Justice" as that which "never speaks the truth"; "The Lady" as "she who has many lovers"; "The Housewife" as "she who has only a few; "Virginity" as "a name denoting nothing." In the original the number of these definitions is greater than what has been translated here for two reasons. First, in some the humor is associated so closely with word-play that it can not be rendered properly in English; second, the medieval openness of Obeyd's language also defies translation.

"Resaleh-ye Delgosha" is a collection of 93 Arabic and 266 Persian anecdotes that have served as vehicles of social and political satire in the hands of the poet. The latter group can be divided into three main categories. First, there are stories that were already popular in Obeyd's time. He often weaves a satirical message into such stories, or they are by themselves satirical: The stories about Sultan Mahmud of Ghazna and his jester Talhak, as well as those related to Juha (or Juhi) the jester, are of this kind. The second category consists of stories related by Obeyd about the personalities who were more or less contemporary with him. Some of these men were forced to play the clown and express their criticism in the form of witticism. Sultan Abu Sa'id, being drunk, forces the great theologian Azud al-Din Iji to dance in front of him. Someone remarks: "O, Mawlana, you are not dancing according to the rules," Azd al-Din retorts: "I dance by decree, not by the rules." In another story the tyrant Atebek Solghur Shah every year transcribes a Qur'an and sends it to Mecca. The poet Majd Hamgar tells him, "You are doing well. You don't even read it. You send it to the house of its Lord!" The third category of satirical anecdotes is composed of stories dealing with the tyranny and corruption of society in a more straightforward way. For example, someone asks the same Azud al-Din: "How is it that in the time of the caliphs people would often claim to be God or a prophet, and now they don't?" He responds, "These days people are so oppressed by tyranny and hunger that they think neither of God nor of the prophets!"

These stories thus graphically depict the social conditions of the time and are among the most remarkable works of Obeyd. Whether preexisting or invented by him, they expose the conditions of the age more accurately than any formal history. Some of the anecdotes may have been of popular origin, representing the injustice that people had experienced. Thus they constitute a contemporary folklore much like that which was evolving during the reign of Mohammad Reza Shah and still is evolving in Iran today under the present regime.

Obeyd displayed a remarkable originality in the forms of satire that he wrote. In addition to "definitions," "maxims" and "short anecdotes" that he uses as vehicles for his satire, one of his most popular poems is in the form of the "animal fable." "Mush u Gorba" (The Mouse and the Cat), which in this volume appears as "Cat and Mouse" in Dick Davis' translation), is a political satire in the form of an animal fable which is at the same time a mock heroic imitation of the *Shahnameh*. Although it is the most well known work of Obeyd and for many years scholars have discussed the political and historical meaning of this ingenious fable, it is hard to say with certainty who were the butts of his satire. Both Masoud Farzad and Abbas Iqbal agree that in many ways the cat resembles the hypocritical and tyrannical Mubarez al-Din Muhammad. His closing of taverns, his pretentious religiosity, and his recognition of the authority of the successor to the Abbasid caliphs in Egypt, all might have induced Obeyd to make him the villain of the poem. Further research reveals that this theory can be more firmly established.

Many characteristics of the cat interestingly enough match those of Mubarez al-Din Muhammad. He was a bully and physically an extraordinarily large man. The historian Hafez Abru (d. 1430) writes: "Amir Mubarez al-Din was very ill-natured, wrathful, foul-mouthed and abusive, and would utter obscenities which even muleteers would be ashamed of uttering."[22] In the fable the cat swears obscenely in Turkish at the mouse whom he has caught behind a wine vat in the tavern, and calls him a "Musulman" in contempt. The cat also swears at the king of the mice in Turkish, who has asked him to come to his capital. It seems that the use of Turkish is also significant as we know that the mother of Mubarez al-Din was a Turkish princess.

R. Homayoun Farrokh, who has made a lengthy study of Hafez, has found some other interesting references to the "cat."[23] According to one historical work of the period, *Matla' al-Sa'dain* by Abdul Razzaq Samarqandi, Mubarez al-Din had no high regard for the valor of his son Shah Shoja and would call him "a worthless cat."[24] Apparently this was one of the idiosyncratic phrases used by Mubarez al-Din. Furthermore, when he was the governor of Yazd in 1319, he fought with a Turkish tribe in Kerman called "Novruzi." In a battle scene, which resembles that of the fable, the horse of Mubarez al-Din is hamstrung, and he is only saved from being captured by one of his generals. Mubarez al-Din kills one of the tribal chiefs and captures another. Strangely enough the latter is nicknamed "the cat" (gorba). He is placed in an iron cage, and, with the head of his slain friend hanging from his neck, he is sent to the Il-Khan Abu Sa'id.[25]

To continue historical reference to the "cat," mention should be made of the poet Hafez. It has been reported that his patron Shah Shoja greatly favored Imad Faqih of Kirman, who was a pretentious Sufi. He had taught his cat to follow him in his genuflections when he performed his prayers. While for the king this achievement was

---

22 Arberry, A. J. *Classical Persian Literature*, George Allen & Unwin, 1958, pp. 298–9.

23 Humayoun Farrokh, *Hafez-i Kharabati*, Tehran, 1976, vol. I, p. 425.

24 Quoted in ibid, pp. 404–34.

25 Quoted in ibid, p. 419.

like a miracle of asceticism for Hafez it was the mere trick of a char-
latan. He says:

> *Sufi hath made display of his virtues and begun*
>   *his blandishments;*
>
> *He hath inaugurated his schemings with the*
>   *juggling heavens.*
>
> *O gracefully-moving partridge who walkest with*
>   *so pretty an air,*
>
> *Be not deceived because the cat of the ascetic hath*
>   *said its prayers.*[26]

It has been reported that a contemporary poet, Imad Faqih,
had taught his cat to follow him in his genuflections when he per-
formed his prayers.[27] The story of this "sanctimonious cat" brings
to mind the cat of Obeyd. The cat eats up the mice and then like a
true "mulla" feels penitent and vows that he will never eat another
mouse. Even in his prayers to God, he "opens the door of decep-
tion and falsehood until he starts weeping." All this reminds us of
Mubarez al-Din. As was mentioned earlier, he cut off the heads of
two prisoners and went on with his prayers as if nothing had hap-
pened. Before he fought some Turkish tribes in Kerman, he first
declared them "heretics" and himself a "ghazi" or defender of Islam.
Earlier in life he drank wine, but in 1351 he repented and became
extremely devout. With all these points, we may safely say that
Obeyd modeled his cat after Mubarez al-Din.

To extend this analogy one step further, we know that Mubarez al-
Din's allegedly heretical foes were three Qara-Khatai tribes between
Yazd and Kerman. They were called Oumani, Jermai and Novruzi.
These tribes are apparently the mice who, because of the tyranny
of the cat, take their case to the king of the mice. Historically, they
complain to Abu Ishaq, who sends two thousand horsemen to fight
Mubarez al-Din. The battle is inconclusive, and Abu Ishaq sends an
"old and well spoken" envoy, who was Imad al-Din Mahmud, a wise
minister and a patron of Hafez, to negotiate a peace treaty. Thus

---

26 Browne, op. cit. p. 280.

27 Hafez, translated by Browne, *A Literary History of Persia*, III, p. 280.

these tribes once more are left at the mercy of Mubarez al-Din. It is in an earlier encounter with these tribes that his horse is hamstrung and, like the cat, he is almost taken captive. But he is saved by one of his generals, Taj al-Din Ali Shah, and eventually the tribesmen are defeated. In Obeyd's poem, the "cat's army marches by the way of the desert" and that of the mice comes from Isfahan, meeting on the plains of Fars. It seems that Obeyd makes these two battles and possibly the last encounter with Abu Ishaq into one battle in which the oppressed come close to victory, but alas it fails them.

To complete the list of Obeyd's writings, mention should be made of three works that are not included in the present volume. Two of them are *Fal-nameh-ye Buruj* (Augury Book of Zodiac Signs) and *Fal-nameh-ye Wuhush va Tuyur* (Augury Book of Animals and Birds). Both are satirical treatments of those who believe in divination of the future and who try to achieve this through different means. The third work is entitled *Rishnameh* (The Book of the Beard), which has been translated by Paul Sprachman in his *Suppressed Persian: An Anthology of Forbidden Literature*. It is a fantastic dialogue between Obeyd and the Beard who is considered the destroyer of youthful beauty. It is written in a style reminiscent of the *Gulistan* of Sa'di (1184–1292) – an almost rhyming prose interspersed with lines of poetry. The style of Obeyd is both beautiful and skillful, but because of various Qur'anic verses and references to cultural peculiarities it loses much of its beauty in translation.

"The Book of the Beard" mainly dwells on the subject of homosexuality and the fact that young and handsome boys had many lovers. In Persian literature the subject has been treated by many poets from Suzani to Sa'di among the classical poets, and from Qa'ani to Iraj Mirza in the times nearer to us. Everybody was aware of it, but no one made an issue out of it. Sa'di typifies the general attitude. He writes in the *Gulistan*, "When young, as it happens and you know, I had an affair with a handsome boy." The love of Mahmud of Ghazna for his favorite slave Ayaz became proverbial, and the attachment of Naser al-Din Shah to his young courtier Malijak inspired many stories. Obeyd with his usual openness and biting humor gives a vivid picture of sexual life in his age. He voices the practice of the age when he says, "Buy young Turkish slaves at whatever price, when they are beardless, but sell them at whatever price when their beards begin to appear." Similarly the twelfth century Ziarid prince Unsur al-Ma'ali in the *Qabus-nama* advises his son on how to buy slaves of both sexes and when to make love to them. The men of the time not only made use of slaves, who had no choice but to submit to the passion of their masters, but also of many handsome boys, who vied with each other in getting more lovers. It seems that "The Book of the Beard" is a light-hearted and witty treatment of the subject, and Obeyd's recommendation is:

"Before the calamity of the Beard strikes, make the best use of your time."

In his other works Obeyd takes a much more critical view of the subject. He is bisexual and very open about it, but what he cannot tolerate is the attitude of people who do the very same thing which they sanctimoniously rebuke others for. Hafez writes:

> *Preachers who on the pulpit such righteousness display,*
> *When in private another game do they play.*
> *Ask this question of the scholar in his teaching bent;*
> *Those who preach repentance, pray why do they not repent?*
> *It is as if they do not believe in the Judgment Day*
> *That in the work of God they cheat and play.[28]*

Here, the other "game" they play does not necessarily mean homosexuality; rather it could be any act that is condemned by hypocritical teachers of morality. Obeyd is full of sarcasm when he says, "When young do not withhold your sexual favors from friends and foes so that in old age you can attain the status of a sheikh, a preacher or a man of fame." Again Hafez says:

> *I am a drinker of wine, a rend and lover of beauties,*
> *Who is not like me in this city? Show me one.[29]*

But the way Obeyd puts the same point is very different:

---

28 See my article, "Tanz va Enteqad dar Dastan-i Hayvanat" in *Alefba IV*,
    Tehran, 1974, pp. 16–18. Also, for a futher discussion of the subject see my *Satire in Persian Literature,* Fairleigh Dickinson University Press, 1988, ch. 5.

29 *Divan-i Hafez,* ed. Parviz Natel Khanlari, Tehran, 1983, vol. 1, p. 404.

"A preacher in Kashan says that on the Day of Judgement, Ali, the cousin of the Prophet, will be in charge of the heavenly well of Kowthar and will give its water to the person who has not slept with a homosexual. A man from Kashan gets up and leaving the mosque says: "O my friend, surely he has to put back the water in the pitcher and drink it all himself!"

Even the inhabitants of the holy city of Qom are not spared by Obeyd.

"Two old gay men from the town, after making love at the top of a minaret – of all places – are talking. One says: "This city of ours is full of corruption." The other answers: "What do you expect from a city whose blessed old men are like us?"

Men of the cloth are favorite objects of ridicule for Obeyd. A preacher is asked, "What is Islam?" He says: "I am a preacher; I have nothing to do with Islam." In another story a preacher's son, who has seen his father having intercourse with their donkey, comes in during a Friday sermon, and innocently asks, "Father, will you service the donkey or shall I take her to graze?"

Lastly a few words should be said about my translation. As was said earlier, the language of Obeyd has a medieval bluntness that in its archaic style does not seem to be offensive. But finding exact English equivalents for some Persian expressions is often impossible. For instance, the expression "service the donkey" in the story above is not as expressive as its Persian original. At the same time some English expressions would have an exaggerated force or undue flavor of class or period. This has been the main problem in the translation. Furthermore, Obeyd often plays with words in ways that are impossible to reproduce in English. In a story he writes, "There was a very tyrannical governor in Mazandaran called Ala. One year there was no rain and people went out to say prayers asking for rain. At the end of his sermon the preacher said: "O God, take from us the calamity, cholera and Ala." In the original the last three words (*balā, vabā*, and *Alā*) rhyme and create an effectiveness that is lost in translation.

Of Obeyd's "The Mouse and the Cat," there are several translations available. Translations by Masoud Farzad (London, 1946), Arberry (1958), Omar Pound (1970), and Basil Bunting (1991), are the most notable. However, I believe that Dick Davis' translation is both graceful and closer to the original, and he has graciously allowed me to reproduce it here. There is an old manuscript of "Mush ve Gorbeh", which has not been included in the Persian editions of Obeyd's works. The variants of this manuscript have been noted in the footnotes of the present volume.

Apart from some translations by E. G. Browne (*A Literary History of Persia*, Cambridge University Press, 1920, pp. 244–57), and a few works mentioned above, the other writings of Obeyd have never appeared in English. It is hoped that, in spite of being only a selection, the present volume may stimulate interest in the works of this talented and ingenious poet and satirist.

Finally, I should mention that the first edition of this book was published in 1985. For this second edition I have replaced Masoud Farzad's translation of "Rats Against Cats" with Dick Davis' "Cat and Mouse." I have also made considerable revisions and added footnotes for Obeyd's references to other poets' works and included English translations of some of these poems. I am grateful to the suggestions of Eric Hooglund, Michael Beard and Farinaz Firouzi who have helped me in the revision of this second edition.

ETHICS OF THE ARISTOCRATS

Infinite thanks and boundless glorification to God Almighty (may His power be exalted), who made the Intellect the ornament of man's existence for him to do his utmost in achieving praiseworthy characteristics and estimable qualities. Incalculable greetings upon the luminous and fragrant sanctuary of the Master of Creation, Mohammad the Chosen One (upon whom be the most perfect salutations), of whose character and life the divine sayings, "Were it not for your sake, We would not have created the firmament,"[1] and "Truly you have an excellent disposition,"[2] are ample glorifications. And peace and salutations be upon his descendants and helpers; "Whosoever of them you follow will lead you to salvation."[3]

To continue, may it not be hidden from the wise, to whom these words are addressed, that in every human body a precious essence from the world divine is in charge and command, whose name is soul, and on whose virtue the Qur'anic verse reads, "Say to them, 'the soul is from the order of my Lord.'"[4] The basis of human existence rests upon this essence which is self-existing, secure from destruction, and inclined to elevation and perfection. As the body lusts after pleasures and turns towards the carnal world, similarly the soul enjoys the familiarity of the Most High, who is the Goal beyond all goals, benefiting from the virtues and comprehending

---

1 A *hadith* in which God tells the Prophet Mohammad: "Were it not for your sake we would not have created the world and the world to come." See Badi al-Zaman Furuzanfar, *Ahadith-i Mathnavi*, Tehran, 1955, p. 172.

2 Qur'an, 68:4.

3 This is a *hadith* reported by Sunni Muslims.

4 Qur'an, 17:85.

the realities, it tends to rise toward the heavenly spheres. As the body falls short of performing its functions because of chronic diseases, the soul also because of its own infirmities – of which there are many, such as love of wealth and position, engrossment with lust and pleasures – is restrained from realizing its nature and quality, which aims at attaining the presence of His Glorious Majesty, understanding the intellects, and gaining purity. Well has the poet said:

> *You are brought forth from the two Worlds*
> *And nurtured by many an intermediary*
> *After the Resurrection, you are that first Intellect*
> *Reckon not yourself as so secondary.*[5]

Just as the physicians have tried their best to cure the illnesses of the body and to maintain its health, so similarly the prophets have striven to remove the ailments and misfortunes of the soul, in order to convey it from the sea of perdition and the whirlpools of ignorance and imperfection, to the shores of safety and perfection. When the man of wisdom looks attentively at the matter, it will become clear that the object of sending those who have been entrusted with prophethood was to refine the character and purify the morals of God's servants. The poet has thus stated the point:

> *Whether the prophet comes or not, make virtue your goal,*
> *For men of virtue to hell will never go.*

The most excellent Prophet has himself unveiled the bride of this idea, and has exposed the beauty of this subtlety. He has said: "I have been sent to complete the virtuous qualities."[6] In order to guide human nature to perfection in the best and safest way, the

---

5 These couplets are from the introduction to Ferdowsi's *Shahnameh*. The "first Intellect" may be referring to the *hadith*, "The first thing that God created was the Intellect." Therefore, although last to be created, man, from the point of possessing the intellect, which is in fact the essence of his existence, is regarded as being foremost among God's creation. See Mohammad Al-Ghazzali, *Ehya Ulum-al-Din*, vol. 1, pg. 37.

6 This *hadith* is attributed to the Prophet Mohammad.

laws of this science, known as "Ethics" or "Practical Philosophy," have been compiled by scholars of the past in lengthy volumes, which the intellect of the present humble author unfortunately fails to grasp. Since the blessed time of Adam the Pure to this day, the noblest of mankind, with great striving, have tried to attain the four major virtues of wisdom, courage, chastity and justice, which they consider the means of happiness in this life and of salvation thereafter. Concerning these they say:

> *Of whatever faith you are, be generous and a doer of good*
> *For unbelief with a good nature is better than Islam*
> *with a bad character.*

Now in this day, which is the best of times and the sum of all centuries, the nature of great men has been refined, and leaders of lofty ideals have appeared who have concentrated their undivided attention and all-embracing thoughts on the affairs of this world as well as the next, and in the eye of their judgment the customs and practices of the ancients have appeared unfounded and contemptible. Since with the passage of time, the lapse of ages, most of these laws had become obsolete, their renovation seemed a burdensome prospect to the powerful minds and bright intellects of these men. Therefore, they trampled those ethical principles and practices under their manly feet, and, for the sake of this life and the next, adopted the methods now practiced among our noblemen and leaders, and regulated their religious and worldly affairs accordingly. A brief account of this will be given in the following pages. And since the door of thought is open and the thread of discourse long, let us therefore begin the matter at hand.

For some time this humble writer, Obey-e Zakani, has been considering writing a short treatise on the ethical principles of the ancients, now called "abrogated," as well as an account of the practices and character of the great men of our time, now considered "adopted" or "approved," for the benefit of the students of this science and the novices of this path. Now, at last, in the year of the Hijra 740 (1339–40 A.D.), I have succeeded in writing this brief account, entitled "Ethics of the Aristocrats."[7] This has been divided into seven chapters, and each chapter contains two practices: first, the "abrogated practice," according to which our ancestors organized their lives, and second, the "adopted practice," which now has been revealed by our leaders and according to which they regulate their affairs in this world and the next. Although this brief account borders on satire, yet

> *He who from familiarity's town doth arise*
> *Knows well the locale of our merchandise.*[8]

The hope of this humble author in composing this short treatise is that

> *Perchance a man of pure soul one day*
> *A prayer for this needy one will say.*[9]

---

7 In Giovanni M. Derme's Italian translation of Obeyd (*Iranica*, Instituto Universitario Orientale, Naples, 1979), the title of the book is translated as "L'Etica dei nobili," and "Akhlagh al-Ashraf" can be translated as "The Manners of the Noble," thus giving a double entendre.

8 This poem is from Nezami (circa 1140–1230).

9 This line comes from the Gulistan of Sa'di (edited by Ghulam Hussein Yousefi, Tehran: Kharazmi, 6th ed., 2002, p. 57). It is an envoi at the end of the introduction of Gulistan where Sa'di asks the reader to pray to God on his behalf. He writes:

> *This well-arranged composition will remain for years,*
> *When every atom of our dust is dispersed.*
> *The intention of this design was that it should survive*
> *Because I perceive no stability in my existence,*
> *Unless one day a pious man compassionately*
> *Utters a prayer for the works of dervishes.*

The *Gulistan*, or, Rose garden of Sa'di / translated by Edward Rehatsek; edited with a preface by W. G. Archer; introduction by G. M. Wickens, New York, Putnam, 1965. It can be assumed that all unidentified quotations and poems in this work are the poet's own as no references to them have been found.

CHAPTER ONE

ON WISDOM

THE ABROGATED PRACTICE

Wise men have thus defined Divine Wisdom: "It aims at the perfec-
tion of the human soul in its powers of learning and practice. The
former is to know the nature of things as they are, and the latter is
to attain the spiritual capacity to enable one to accomplish good
deeds and avoid works of evil, and this is called ethics."[10] This is to
say that two faculties are concentrated in a rational being, and his
perfection depends on their perfection. One is the faculty of specu-
lation and the other, that of practice. The speculative faculty is that
which yearns to acquire learning and knowledge by virtue of which
it will obtain the capacity for knowing things as they truly are. Thus
man will be ennobled by knowledge of the True Goal and the Ulti-
mate Aim – may He be exalted and sanctified – which is the destiny
of all beings, and being guided by such a knowledge, he may attain
the World of Oneness or perhaps the Station of Union to assuage
and soothe his heart.[11] "Verily with the invocation of God's name
hearts become tranquil"[12] and the dust of doubt and the rust of
uncertainty are rubbed from the mirror of his thought. The poet has
said:

Wherever certitude has arrived, doubt has fled.

The faculty of practice correlates one's power and deeds in such a
way that they harmonize with each other, so that as a result of this
harmony and balance one's character becomes worthy of praise. If a
man combines knowledge and practice to this extent, he is called a
perfect man and the deputy of God on earth, and his rank will be
highest amongst mankind. As God Almighty has said: "He bestows
wisdom on whomsoever He wills, and he to whom is given wisdom

---

10 These lines are in Arabic. Obey-e Zakani mockingly adopts the high-flown style of
Muslim philosophers and brings in many Arabic quotations.

11 For the different stages (or maqamat) of Sufism, see A. J. Arberry's Sufism. New
York: George Allen and Anne Unwin Ltd., 1950.

12 Qur'an, 13:28.

has been given a great blessing."[13] After departure from the body the soul of such a person will be fit for everlasting happiness, eternal bounty, and Divine grace.

> *This is the work of Fate may it fall upon whom it will.*[14]

Thus far we have been discussing the ways of the ancients and the philosophers.

THE ADOPTED PRACTICE

When the great and wise men whose existence honors the face of the earth pondered over the human soul, its origin and its destiny, and when they weighed the beliefs and practices of the great men of the past, they categorically rejected the entirety of these beliefs. They profess that it has been revealed to us that the rational soul in itself is of little value, and that its existence is dependent upon bodily existence, and its extinction upon bodily extinction. They also declare that what the prophets have said concerning the rational soul, that it never diminishes or increases and after departure from the body it will continue to subsist through its own essence, is impossible. Likewise, the idea of resurrection is an absurd supposition. Life is the result of the harmony of bodily elements, and when the body decays the man is destroyed forever. The supposed joys of heaven and the sufferings of hell exist in this world. As the poet has said:

> *The well-to-do has only today and what is here*
> *While the have-not has tomorrow as his share.*[15]

Thus necessarily their minds are entirely unperturbed by the thought of resurrection, future punishment, proximity to or remote-

---

13 Qur'an, 2:269.

14 This line is from Seyyed Hasan Ghaznavi (d. 1160) *Divan*, Modarres Razavi, p. 48.

15 That is to say, there is no future life. The editors of Obeyd have not been able to find the source of this poem. E. G. Browne translates it as:
    He to whom they give receives his gift even here,
    And he who has nothing [here] is put off with promises for "tomorrow."
    (*A Literary Hisory of Persia*, vol. III, p. 248.)

ness from God, divine favor or wrath, perfection or imperfection; and as a result of their convictions they spend their lives lusting after sensual delights. They say:

> *You who are resulted from four and seven,* [16]
> *And always suffer from seven and four,*
> *Drink wine for I've told you, aye, thousands of times,*
> *That's all: when you're gone, you're no more.*

They often have the following quatrain inscribed upon the coffins of their forefathers:

> *Beyond this rotary vault, no arch or mansion lies:*
> *None has wisdom or perception except for you and I*
> *You that something of this nothing have thought*
> *Pass by this fantasy for it exists not.*

It is because of this belief, they have not the least regard for the life, property and the honor of people.

> *Dearer to him is a wine cup of fire's colors*
> *Than the crimson blood of one hundred brothers.* [17]

Indeed, they are great masters of success, and what was veiled and hidden for thousands of years from many men, despite their purification of soul and intellect, was easily revealed to them.

---

16 Mankind was believed to be the outcome of four elements and the working of the seven heavens. Cf. *Rubaiyyat-i Omar Khayyam*, Lucknow edition of 1312, A.H., No.723:

> Child of four elements and the sevenfold heaven,
> Who fume and sweat because of these eleven,
> Drink! I have told you seventy times and seven,
> Once gone, neither hell will send you back nor heaven.

(*The Quatrains of Omar Khayyam*, tr. E. H. Whinfield, London, 1883, No. 431.)

17 Obeyd's editors have been unable to find the source of this poem. One can assume it is Obeyd's own.

CHAPTER TWO

ON COURAGE

THE ABROGATED PRACTICE

OBEYD-E
ZAKANI

Philosophers have said: The human soul has three distinct powers, from which issue forth various actions. First is the power of speech, which is the source of thought and understanding. Second is the choleric power, which leads to an urge to take chances, and a desire for supremacy. Third is the power of concupiscence, also called the animal power, from which comes the desire for food, drink and marriage. If the rational soul is in equilibrium in a person and he has an enthusiasm for learning certainties, he will tread the path of wisdom. Whenever the animal or choleric humor is in equilibrium and submissive to the rational soul, the virtue of courage will come forth, and whenever the movement of the animal nature is in equilibrium and follows the rational soul, the virtue of chastity will emerge. When these three virtues are produced and intermingled the result is the most perfect of virtues and is called the sense of justice. Philosophers have called a person courageous who possesses these qualities: chivalry, high aspiration, tranquility, steadfastness, forbearance, courage, humility, ardor and compassion. One who is characterized by the virtue of courage is praised, exalted, and stands without shame among men. Thus the pearls of his valor and exploits in battle have been strung on the thread of poetry, and the poet has said:

> *The capital of man is manliness,*
> *Bravery, chivalry and wisdom.*

THE ADOPTED PRACTICE

Our contemporaries[18] have said that a person who commits the horrifying act of facing another man in combat confronts one of two conditions: either he overcomes his opponent and kills him, or else he is killed. If he kills the enemy, he has shed an innocent man's

---

18 Obeyd uses the word "*as-habena*" which can mean "our contemporaries" or "our friends" and he sarcastically alludes to those in power who claim that manliness and good character are antiquated.

blood, and in consequence he will sooner or later follow his victim. And if the foe overcomes him, again he will follow the path to hell. How should a wise man undertake an action having such potential ends? What proof is better than this, that whenever there is a wedding, a feast or gathering with food, sweetmeats, robes of honor and money, then eunuchs, rogues, lute-players, and men of lusty disposition will seek it out. But whenever there is a battlefield with swords and spears, they will look for a fool to prop up facing the blades, and they will call him a real man, a hero, a destroyer of armies and a knight of valor. When the unfortunate man is killed, the lechers, eunuchs and effeminates of the town will waggle their hips and reproachfully say:

> *I won't be hit by an arrow, axe, spear, or the rest,*
> *Delicate food, wine and minstrels suit me best.*

When a warrior is killed in battle, eunuchs and effeminates who have watched from a distance, say to him, "O dear master, live in shame, but live long." The man of prudence in time of war must follow the maxim of the knights from Khorasan, who said, "Brave men dash onto the battlefield, but we dash into a barn of straw!" This is why the knights of our time have this line engraved on their signet rings:

> *Fleeing in time is a true victory,*
> *Happy the knight who has such a destiny.*

It has been related that an upstart man from Isfahan encountered a Mongol soldier in the wilderness. When the Mongol attacked him the prudent youth humbly said: "O master, for God's sake do me, but do not do me in!"[19] The Mongol took pity on him, and did as he had asked. I was told that the young man who was saved through this stratagem lived in great honor and esteem for thirty years. O what a fortunate young man! It seems that the following proverb has been said of him:

---

19 The expression is originally in the Isfahani dialect: "Ay Agah Khoda ra bem gam mam kosh," which means, "Please rape me but don't kill me."

As for the bright and wise youths,
It is fitting, if they sit on top of the old.

O friends, take heed of the manners and customs of these great men. How unfortunate were our ancestors who lived out their lives in ignorance and whose minds never perceived such great ideas!

CHAPTER THREE

ON CHASTITY

THE ABROGATED PRACTICE

I have read in the biographies of the great men of the past that they regarded chastity as one of the four virtues and defined it as "purity." Chaste was a person who kept his eyes from seeing the unlawful, his ears from hearing gossip, his hands from seizing the property of others, his tongue from uttering unseemly words, and his soul from carrying out evil deeds. Such a person was respected and endeared, as the poet has said:

One who is virtuous, honest of hand and of the utmost sincerity,
Will stand high amongst the people like a cypress tree.

This point is exemplified by the following story. It has been related that a wise man, having heard his son criticizing someone, said: "O my son, why do you allow a fault upon your tongue, which you do not approve of on the body of another person?" A man was complaining of another man and was vilifying him before the Leader of the Faithful, Hasan ibn Ali.[20] The Commander of the Faithful said to his son, "Keep your ear away from his speech, lest what is most wicked in his vessel may pour into yours." When Mansur al-Hallaj was being crucified, he said: "When I was a boy, I was playing along a street and heard the voice of a woman from a roof top. In order to

---

20 Imam Hasan was the grandson of Mohammad and the son of Imam Ali. After the assassination of his father in 661 AD, Hasan became the caliph, but before long he lost his position to his rival Mu'awiyya, and retired to Medina where nine years later he was poisoned and died.

see her I wantonly turned and looked up at her. Now looking down from the cross is a punishment for that looking up."[21]

THE ADOPTED PRACTICE

Our masters say that the ancients have made a grave mistake on the subject and have wasted their precious lives in ignorance and error. Whoever follows this path can never enjoy his life. The text of the Revealed Book reads: "Know that the present life is but a sport and diversion, an adornment and a cause for boasting among you, and a rivalry in wealth and children."[22] They have interpreted this to mean that it is impossible to enjoy life without playing and indulging in vices and forbidden pleasures. Likewise it is not feasible to amass a fortune without hurting and tyrannizing people, and gossiping or lying about them. Whoever is virtuous will inevitably be deprived of all these blessings and cannot be counted amongst the living, as his life would be considered wasted. He must be held responsible according to this verse of the Qur'an, which says: "What, did you think that We created you in vain, and that you would not return to Us?"[23] What an insanity if a man be alone with a moonlike beauty, and on the grounds of chastity to refuse her soul-reviving embrace, and forever regret the occasion. It is quite possible that such an opportunity might never occur again up to the end of his days, and his life-long regret might cause his death, as he says: "Missing an opportunity brings sorrow!" A person once described as a pious, virtuous, and self-controlled man would now be called a jackass, frigid and a complete failure. Our teachers argue that the eyes, tongue and other members of the body are made to attract benefit and defy loss.

---

21 Husain Ibn Mansur Hallaj was the great Iranian Sufi who was executed in Baghdad in 922 on account of his outwardly heretical and pantheistic sayings. For his life see E. G. Browne, *A Literary History of Persia*, I, p. 428 et seq.

22 Obeyd quotes the Qur'anic verse out of context reversing the intent in order to prove his point. The actual text, referring to heavenly rewards in the next world, is "Know that this present life is only a toy and a vain amusement; and worldly pomp, and the affection of glory among you, and the multiplying of riches and children are as the plants nourished by the air. The springing up whereof delights the husbandmen, afterwards they wither, so that thou seest the same turn yellow, and at length become dry stubble." Qur'an, 57:20.

23 Qur'an, 23:115

Thus, if one deprives a member of the function for which it has been created, one has wasted it. Since it is not permissible to waste the members of one's own body, one must watch whatever pleases one's eyes, hear whatever delights one's ears, and utter whatever conforms to one's interest such as vilifying, molesting, gossiping, backbiting, swearing blatantly, and giving false testimony. If as a result the house of another person is ruined or he otherwise suffers, one should hold one's thought above such pettiness. Do and say whatever you please, and sleep with whomever you please without any scruple, so that your life may not be burdensome.

> *As much as possible seek to find*
> *A sweetheart-graceful, playful, and refined.*
> *When you have found her, waste no time.*
> *Have her, leave her, then make another thine.*

It is said if a master or a friend is expecting to enjoy a certain person, that person should accept it without hesitation and without making excuses. As the saying goes, "Opportunity passes as the clouds."

> *Let not today's affair until tomorrow go;*
> *Of what will come tomorrow who can ever know?*[24]

One has to bear in mind that "forbidding is a heresy." It is common knowledge that if men or women did not make themselves available and indulge in intercourse, they would be distressed, anguished, and will bear the brunt of their wasted desire forever. It has also been proven since the time of Adam the Pure that whoever was not sodomized did not become an emir, a vizier, a pahlavan, a mighty warrior, a man of great wealth and fortune, or a well-known courtier, sheikh or Sufi. Hence the Sufi saying that being sodomized is an "ailment of the sheikhs."[25] As I heard a great man advise his son:

---

24 A proverb from a poem by Ferdowsi in the *Shahnameh* (Brokheem Ed., vol. ii, line 1191). For a new translation of the *Shahnameh* see, *Shahnameh: The Persian Book of Kings,* translated by Dick Davis, Mage Publishers, 2004.

25 The original "illat al-mashayikh" (ailment of the Sheikhs) presumably refers to some corrupt Sufi sheikhs. Obeyd, in his definitions, also refers this ailment (ibna) as "illat-i-akaber" (ailment of the great). The term ibna refers to someone who has been sexually used.

Strive to be generous from the rear,

That from your charity success appear.

It has been recorded in histories that Rostam son of Zal achieved all his greatness in this manner. It has been said:

When Rostam had undone his drawers

He knelt down, the hero of many wars.

As Gudarz had taught him at night

Houman made his pillar upright

He rammed into Rostam in such a way

That he thought his back will give away.

Then was Houman's turn to lie down

And Rostam like a lion mounted on

Harder and harder into him he lanced

That Houman's back was badly marred.

Two swordsmen were sorely torn

But amongst the brave became well known.

You too my brother, when strong and great

Will be well advised, to hear my words straight.

To lie prone, hold up your rear part,

And display all your good art.

So that whoever comes may lie with you

And no regrets or qualms will be left for you.

As our stay in the world's so short, we find

'Tis best that you leave only good behind.[26]

And also it has been said,

Eternal happiness lies in the game of lovemaking

Give in and you will win; the prize is for taking.

---

26 This part is a description of a homosexual encounter between two heroes of the *Shahnameh* and a parody of the style of Ferdowsi but in a coarse language. For a different translations of this passage see, Paul Sprachman, *Suppressed Persian: An Anthology of Forbidden Literature* (Mazda Publishers, Costa Mesa, 1995), p. 58, also Robert Surieu's *Sarv-e Naz: An Essay on Love and Representation of Erotic Themes in Ancient Iran* (Nagel Publishers: Geneva, 1967), pp. 127–28, which was used in part..

In truth our great men have said from experience, and truth is on their side, that it has been proven that chastity is not auspicious. Man has to be enjoyed and enjoy himself – as the system of the world's affairs is that of give and take – so that he may be called great and noble from both sides.[27] And if his parents have been givers in this way, he can be called of good pedigree. Though some common people have claimed that being sodomized is a form of "reverse generosity," their claim has no value because they don't know that "Self sacrifice is utmost generosity." Whoever because of misfortune loses his opportunity and misses the key to fortune, he will remain in despair and adversity forever. And so the poet has said:

> *Lamenting he bit his hand*
> *The man who did not bake*
> *When a hot oven was at hand.*[28]

This much will suffice for the fortunate man whose nature is willing to accept good advice. May God Almighty bless us all.

CHAPTER FOUR

ON JUSTICE

THE ABROGATED PRACTICE

The great men of the past regarded justice as one of the four virtues, and upon it they based the foundation of this world and the next. Their belief was that "By justice the heavens and the earth stand upright,"[29] and they wanted to obey the message of the Qur'an which says, "God orders you to practice justice and be generous."[30]

---

27 Obeyd uses the phrase in two ways, one is the outer meaning of double lineage "from both the father's and mother's side," and the other is a tongue-in-cheek reference to one who engages in sexual intercourse in "both ways."

28 This poem is from the first chapter of *Bustan* of Sa`di (*Kulliyyat*, Furughi ed., p. 226). A sage advises the king of Rome (Rum) to make most of his time and leave a good name before it is too late.

29 A *hadith*.

30 Qur'an, 16:90.

Therefore, the kings, emirs and noblemen always tried to be just and to look after their subjects and soldiers as the means for attaining good repute. They so firmly believed in this that they encouraged the common people to be just in their dealings and partnerships and said:

> *Be just since in the heart's own lands*
> *The just the Prophet's state commands.[31]*

THE ADOPTED PRACTICE

But the view of our contemporaries is that this quality is the worst of all attributes and that justice brings forth much loss, a thesis that they have proved with the clearest of proofs. They say: "Punishment is the bulwark of kingship, lordship and mastership." Unless a man is feared no one will obey his orders, and all will feel themselves equals. Thus the order of affairs will be disrupted and the administration will be undermined. One who practices justice – God forbid – and refrains from beating, killing, and fining his subjects, and who does not get drunk and make an uproar and quarrel with them, will not be feared by anyone. Such kings will not be obeyed by their subjects, and children and slaves will not heed the words of their parents and masters. Consequently, the affairs of the country will lapse into chaos. This is why they have said:

> *Kings for gaining one of their objects*
> *Will sacrifice one hundred subjects.[32]*

They say: "Justice bequeaths adversity." What proof can be more convincing than this: that as long as the kings of Iran, such as Zahhak the Arab[33] and Yazdigird the Sinner,[34] who along with the

---

31 This poem is by Anvari, a Saljuk poet and astrologer (d. 1189–91), *Hidiqat-ul-Haqiqah*, (Muddress ed.), p.553.

32 This line is also by Anvari (*Divan*, Moddarres ed.) p. 626.

33 Zahhak or Azhi Dahaka is the evil king of the *Shahnameh* who was brought to the throne by the devil. When the devil kissed him on the shoulders, two serpents grew from each of them and they had to be fed by human brains every day. Historically, Zahhak was the son of Mardas, a king of one of the regions in Arabia, and he came to the throne after Jamshid, the first Iranian king.

34 Yazdigird I of the Sasanian dynasty (339–420) was an energetic and intelligent

other potentates that arrived after them and now honor the best seats in hell, practiced injustice, their kingdoms prospered and flourished. But when the time of Khosrow Anushiravan[35] arrived, he followed the counsel of feeble-minded ministers and chose the way of justice. Before long the pinnacles of his palace fell to the ground and the sacred fire in the temples, which were their places of worship, was extinguished, and all traces of their existence vanished from the surface of the earth. The caliph of the faithful and the establisher of the laws of religion, Umar ibn Khattab[36] – may God rest his soul – was well-known for his justice, used to make bricks and eat barley bread, and as they relate, his [patch-work] robe weighed seventeen mans[37]; whereas Mu'awiyya[38], by virtue of his injustice, usurped the kingdom from Ali – may God enoble his face. Nebuchadnezzar did not establish himself as a king and was not exalted in both worlds, until he murdered twelve thousand innocent prophets in Jerusalem and enslaved several thousand more. Chengiz Khan, who now despite his enemies is the leader and guide of all the Mongols, ancient and modern, in the deepest compartments of hell, did not attain the rulership of the whole world until he shed the blood of thousands and thousands of people.

Zoroastrian ruler who sought to put an end to the persecution of the followers of other sects. He was opposed by Zoroastrian clerics and some of his own chiefs. In the Persian tradition he is consequently known as "the Sinner." Obeyd may not have known of Yazdigird's qualities and thought this title appropriately given.

35 Khosraw or Chosroes I (531–379) surnamed Anushiravan "the Blessed" or "Just," according to Persian tradition. However, this is a misnomer, as he was not a particularly just king. As the crown prince toward the end of his father's reign, he massacred, with the help of the chief Magian priest, a large number of followers of Mazdak, a contemporary religious reformer (in 528 CE). In the time of Obeyd the pre-Islamic history of Iran was little known and consequently he follows the well-known traditions of his time. More about Anushiravan is provided in the notes to "One Hundred Maxims".

36 Umar ibn Khattab, the second successor of the Prophet Mohammad.

37 A man is a Persian measurement whose weight is equivalent to about three kilograms.

38 For Mu'awiyya, see the notes to the "Arabic Stories."

It has been related in Mongol histories that when Hulagu Khan conquered Baghdad he ordered all the inhabitants who had escaped the sword to assemble in front of him. Then he asked each class about its circumstances and after learning about them all, he said: "The artisans are indispensable and should be allowed to go to their work." The merchants were provided with capital so that they could trade for him. Considering the Jews as an oppressed people, he was content with a poll-tax from them. He also sent the eunuchs back to their jobs in order to look after their seraglios. Then he separated the judges, sheikhs, Sufis, Hajis, preachers, noblemen, Seyyeds,[39] beggars, religious mendicants, wrestlers, poets and story-tellers from the rest, and said, "These are superfluous creatures who wrongfully waste the bounty of God." By ordering them all to be drowned in the Tigris, he purified the earth of their vile existence.

Consequently, sovereignty was firmly established in his family for about ninety years, and their prosperity increased every day. But since the poor Abu Sa'id was obsessed with the idea of justice and distinguished himself with this quality, before long the days of his monarchy were numbered, and the House of Hulagu and his endeavors disappeared through the aspirations of Abu Sa'id.[40] It is true to say:

> *When the time of man begins to pale*
> *All his efforts are of no avail.*[41]

Blessings be upon these great and successful men who guided mankind from the dark delusion of justice into the light of proper direction.

---

39 Seyyeds are people descended from the Prophet or the Imams.

40 Abu Sa'id Bahador Khan (d. 1335) was the last king of the House of Hulagu.

41 This is a well-known proverb from the *Shahnameh*.

CHAPTER FIVE

ON GENEROSITY

THE ABROGATED PRACTICE

Trusted sources have noted that people in ancient times admired generosity, and one who was characterized by this quality was praised and glorified. They encouraged their children to be generous. They believed in this to such an extent that if someone fed a hungry person or clad a naked one, or helped one in distress, he was not ashamed. They went to such an extent, in upholding this trait that people not only did not disparage someone generous but praised and admired him. The learned wrote books to glorify his name and the poets eulogized him. This point can be proved by the clear verses (of the Qur'an): "One who brings forth a good deed is rewarded ten times more,"[42] and "You will not attain goodness until you have given away what you have."[43] Also, the Blessed Prophet is related to have said: "The generous will not enter hellfire, even though he be a sinner."[44]

A dear friend has said concerning the subject:

Bind your heart to generosity, if it is greatness that you seek;
Bind your purse loosely with the delicate leaf of leek.

THE ADOPTED PRACTICE

When the great men of our times, who have distinguished themselves by virtue of their strong reasoning and keen perception from the sages of the past, pondered over this subject, their sharp minds perceived the shortcomings of generosity. Therefore, they have hoarded wealth and tried to enjoy the best in life, and have taken these Qur'anic verses as their motto: "Eat and drink but be

---

42 Qur'an, 6:160.

43 Qur'an, 3:92.

44 A *hadith* attributed to Mohammad.

not wasteful,"[45] for "Truly God does not love the extravagant."[46] It became evident to them that it was due to generosity and such extravagance that ancient families came to ruin. One who is known for munificence will never rest in peace. From every side the greedy will seize him and rob him of his wealth with flattery and other pretenses. That unfortunate good-hearted man will be elated by vanity on account of their nonsensical tales and will soon squander his wealth – acquired and inherited – only to become destitute and disillusioned. But the person who is protected by the quality of miserliness would be safe in the refuge of avarice from the evil intentions and insistence of beggars, and would live in bounty and plenitude far away from bothersome people. Our contemporaries put wealth on the same plane as life itself, saying: "Since one's precious life is spent in the pursuit of wealth, it would be unwise to waste it, for instance, on clothing, drinking, eating, on any bodily comfort, or in the pursuit of flattery." Consequently, if a great man has left some money to his heirs, not even with a thousand pincers can a single penny be extracted from their claws, even should the entire kingdoms of India and Rome be his bequest:

> Even if the press stone which from seeds their oil extracts
> Were to press upon his belly, his wind would remain intact.

Also the following lines are appropriate here:

> Lest he hears the word "to part,"
> He will die of colic ere letting a fart.

ANECDOTE

One of the great men of our time told his son, "O my son, know that the word 'No' averts calamity, whereas 'Yes' increases misfortune." Another has said, "O my son, close your ears to the word "Aye" and utter nothing but "Nay", because your prosperity will be high with "Nay", whereas "Aye" brings tears to your eye.

---

45 Qur'an, 7:31.

46 Qur'an, 6:141.

One of the great men, a Croesus of his time, lay on his deathbed, any hope of life severed. He summoned his dear ones who were the children of the House of Generosity, and said: "O children, a long time have I suffered and toiled in search of wealth at home and abroad, and I have pressed my throat with the grip of hunger in order to collect these few golden dinars. Never be neglectful of guarding them, and under no circumstances spend them. As they have said:

Gold is a dear creation of God;
Whoever debases it will be debased.

If someone tells you that he has seen your father in a dream asking for sweetmeats to be given in the way of charity, never believe him, for I have not said it, and a dead man will never eat. Even if I myself appear in a dream and make such a request, pay no heed, and consider it nothing but a dream. Perhaps a demon has assumed my shape. What I have not eaten in my life I should not request after my death." He uttered these words and gave up his soul to the guardian of hell.

ANECDOTE

It has been said of another great man that in dealing with someone he haggled beyond reason over the value of two silver grains. He was told that such a trivial amount is not worthy of such a refusal. He said: "How can I dispense with some of my own property, which suffices me for one day, or a week, or a month, or a year or even for the rest of my life?" When asked, "How can this be?" he said, "If I buy salt with it, it will be enough for one day. If I go to the public bath, it will be enough for a week. If given to a blood-letter, it will suffice for a month. If a broom is bought with it, it will last for a year. If I buy a nail, it will last me a lifetime. Why then should I give away the money through sheer negligence which can attend to so many needs?"

OBEYD-E
ZAKANI

ANECDOTE

It has been said of a great man that when bread was being baked in his house, he would take the loaves one by one in his unblessed hands and say:

May you remain safe from any harm!

Then he would entrust the loaf to his butler. When the smell of the baked bread reached his servants, they would say:

You are behind the veil and our hearts do bleed,
O what will happen if from the veil you are freed?

ANECDOTE

Not long ago a nobleman's son gave his robe to a beggar. His critics informed his father, and he reproached his son. The son said, "I have read in a book that one who wishes greatness on others must his wealth bestow. It was because of this that I gave away my robe." The father said: "O foolish boy, you are mistaken, for that was a misprint for 'stow'.[47] The wise have said, 'You should store whatever you have, if you wish to attain greatness.' Don't you see that great men of our time are forever hoarding?"[48] The poet has said:

Little by little it becomes more,
Grain by grain it fills the store.[49]

ANECDOTE

Another nobleman of our time said to his slave: "Buy a chicken with your own money and prepare a dish from it. I will eat it and set you free." The slave was happy, and prepared a fried chicken. The master

---

47 Obeyd is making a play on the words that can not be translated properly. *Ithar* (ایثار) means to give away and liberality, whereas *anbar* (انبار) means hording. The two words are written in a very similar manner, the only difference being that one has three dots and the other two.

48 Here Obeyd is referring to those who stockpile in order to sell at high prices in times of famine.

49 This is a famous line by Sa'di in the *Gulistan* (chapter 8, Furughi edition, p. 193), which has become a proverb.

51

ate and gave some of it to the slave. The following day he told him, "Add some chick peas and saffron to it. I will eat it and set you free." The slave obeyed and prepared a dish. The master gobbled it up and gave some to the slave. The next day the meat had gone to pieces and was of no use. He said: "Sell this meat and get some butter and make it into another dish. I will eat it and set you free." The slave said, "O master, for the sake of God, let me remain in your servitude, but if you have any good intentions, set the chicken free."

Truly great and prudent is the man who can be so cautious in spending. So long as he lives he will be held dear and everyone will be in need of him. And in the world to come the exaltation of his status will be beyond description.

CHAPTER SIX

FORBEARANCE[50]

THE ABROGATED PRACTICE

Forbearance comes from patience. The ancients have called a man forbearing whose carnal self has gained tranquility and serenity, such that wrath cannot easily stir it up. If an unpleasant event befalls him, he is not agitated. It has been related from his holiness the Prophet: "Forbearance is the veil of misfortunes." If read backwards, *hilm* (forbearance) will become *milh* (salt or grace), and hence the saying: *al-hilm milh al-akhlaq* – "Forbearance is the salt (or charm) of one's character." The poet has thus praised the forbearance of his patron:

---

50 In some versions, the title of this chapter is *"Helm* (forbearance) and *Vafa* (fidelity)". However, in most recent editions, it is only forbearance. It is possible that *vafa* is a copyist error for *viqar* (dignity). Since "fidelity" only appears in the title and is never repeated in the whole chapter, Christensen argues that the word must have been "dignity." Furthermore, *vafa* is one of the subjects treated in the seventh chapter (See "Remarques sur les facéties de ʿUbid-i-Zakani," Acta Orientala, vol. 1, part 1, p. 1).

The burden of your forbearance
Has broke the mountain's back,
So that it stands fixed in place
Like one with affliction racked.
It is so when two consonants collide
That one must break and the other override.[51]

THE ADOPTED PRACTICE

It is true that our contemporaries do not reject this characteristic completely. They say, "Although if one practices forbearance or displays patience, people will treat him with impunity and consider it a sign of weakness. Nonetheless, this characteristic has some value." The proof of the argument is that one who has borne the weight of rogues and sodomites in his youth and who has displayed forbearance and dignity in this respect, now in the parties and gatherings of great men will not be subjected to much mistreatment. They won't slap him on the face, or pluck his beard, or finger him on the back, or throw him into the pond and speak disrespectfully of his wife and sister.

Had not such a wise man, known as the ideal man of our time, born those sufferings with the aid of the forbearance and dignity with which his rational soul was endowed, he could not have gained such great results. He would always have been distressed, wretched and in an evil plight. People would not admit him into their homes, and no great man would honor him. This is why they say, "Impudence is the key to success." The meaning of the following couplet also emphasizes the foregoing fact:

In the mill of life a wise man learns
To be steady under the stone that turns.[52]

---

51 In Persian two consonants cannot occur at the beginning of a syllable. When this happens, the first or second consonant must be followed by a vowel.

52 This is a proverb coming from Sa'di's satirical works (Kulliyyat, Hazaliyyat with introduction of Abbas Iqbal, p. 28) .

One of the advantages of forbearance is as follows: If the harem and retinue of a prominent man be accused of infidelity, and if he is bereft of the ornament of forbearance and dignity, fury will overwhelm his constitution and he will go mad. As they have said, "Anger is the demon of the intellect." He will beat and kill his wife and children and mutilate his servants until, by his own hands, he brings ruin upon his family, earning the contempt of his wife and children. Day and night he will be grief-stricken and thoughtful lest a critic breathes a word of censure about his household, and says:

> *If you have a sense of honor,*
> *You won't escape distress;*
> *If you have no sense of honor,*
> *You will lose your manliness.*[53]

But the blessed minds of those dignified and successful men will not be disturbed in the least if all the members of their families be raped in front of their eyes one thousand times. Therefore, as long as such men live, they will enjoy peace of mind and tranquility. Pleased with their kindred and completely self-assured, they will never heed an accusation, saying rather:

> *If a dog barks at the roof of the barn grieve not.*

ANECDOTE

I heard that one of the noblemen of our time had a chaste but ugly wife. He was saved from her by divorce and took in marriage a beautiful prostitute. The lady, as it is the custom, denounced him everywhere. They reproached him, saying: "Having left a chaste wife, you have chosen a prostitute instead." The nobleman with forbearance and perfect dignity, said: "Your imperfect wisdom can never comprehend such a matter. Formerly I was eating dirt alone, but now I am eating halvah with one thousand men." It is a proverb that "The cuckold is happy in both worlds." The interpretation is that not being afflicted with the disease of honor, he will live in peace both in this world and in the world to come. According to the tradition

53 This is a line from *Khosrow va Shirin* (Vahid Dastgirdi ed. P. 197) of Nezami when he is talking of the relationship between men and women.

"No cuckold will enter heaven," he will neither be bothered by the company of ascetics and sheikhs nor by their long and disagreeable faces. Whenever he sees a sheikh he will say:

If you have a place in heaven,
The others will choose hell[54]

For this reason the cuckold is happy in both worlds. But the point might be raised here: If someone asks, "The cuckold hates going to heaven because of the company of the sheikhs, but he will be similarly opposed to going to hell; because for every sheikh here, there are one thousand judges along with their deputies and lawyers. How is it that he will not be annoyed by their association?" We answer: "Since the sheikhs were well-known for their cleanliness and devotion in this world (though this was never free from hypocrisy and pretension), and since the poor cuckold has never purified himself properly or prostrated himself in prayer, their states will be diametrically opposed to each other. But judges and their followers are well-known for their trickery, deception, usury, sinfulness, injustice, calumny, and fault-finding, as well as bearing false witness, and falsification of the rights of Muslims. Their greed and avidity, their working mischief amongst the people, and their being shameless and accepting bribes have no limits. Since similar qualities are inherent in a cuckold's nature, they could arrive at full accord. It is because of this homogeneity that the cuckold will be inclined to the company of judges and their dependents. It has been said, 'Everyone seeks out his own kind.'" Moreover, it has become proverbial that "Homogeneity is the cause of attraction." Consequently, when the fire-blazers of hell drag such a man to their domain, he will say in self-praise:

If tomorrow they take me to heaven
With the pious but without a friend
Together with the sinners in hell
Would be my preference in the end[55]

---

54 This poem is from Sa'di's *Gulistan*, chapter 5, Furughi ed. p. 133. It comes from the story of "The Parrot and the Crow," which pertains to the incompatibility of their companionship.

55 This is a line from a *ghazal* by Sa'di (*Kulliyat*, ed. Furughi, p. 579).

As one of the great commentators has said of the Qur'anic verse, "There is not one of you but shall pass [the bridge of Sirat]."[56] All people will pass over the bridge of Sirat as swiftly as lightning, except for the judges and their followers, who will remain in hell forever and who will play a fiery game of chess with each other.

It has been recorded in the traditions of the Prophet: "The people of hell play with fire." It is for this reason that such men prefer this attribute to other characteristics.

CHAPTER SEVEN

MODESTY, FIDELITY, SINCERITY, MERCY AND COMPASSION

THE ABROGATED PRACTICE

Sages have said: "Modesty is the restraining of the carnal soul from committing blameworthy acts of obscenity." The Prophet, upon whom be peace, has said, "Modesty comes from faith." Fidelity requires one to tread the way of fellowship, and return what another has done for him. The Qur'anic verse reads, "Whoever fulfills his promise to God will be given a great reward."[57] Sincerity is to be of one heart with friends, so that nothing untruthful will be uttered. In the case of mercy and compassion, if one person sees another in an unfortunate situation, he will be moved to pity and try to change it.

THE ADOPTED PRACTICE

Our contemporaries say, "These qualities are extremely hollow and disagreeable." Whoever is afflicted with one of these fatal qualities will always be dejected and unfortunate and unable to attain any goal. It is self evident that a shy or modest person will be deprived of all good things, and will be unable to gain glory or wealth. Between him and his goal, modesty is a great barrier or a thick veil, and he

---

56 Qur'an, 19:71. This is one of the difficult verses of the Qur'an and some commentators believe that the pronoun "it" in "there is not one of you but shall come to it" refers to hell, and some believe it refers to the bridge of Sirat. In Islamic tradition, Sirat is the bridge across hell that leads to heaven.

57 Qur'an, 48:10.

will forever weep over his misfortune and fate. This is why in Arabic the weeping of a cloud is also called "haya" (modesty or bashfulness). The Prophet – upon whom be peace – has said, "Bashfulness is an obstacle in the way of livelihood."

Anyone who is shameless and impudent is willing to flay anyone, says whatever he desires, and does not give a hoot about anyone. He passes all barriers in order to reach his goal, and snubs his masters and his elders, nay even his lovers. People will fear him because of his impudence. But the unfortunate man who is known for his modesty will be left behind doors, and in waiting rooms he will be beaten by the ushers, and enviously watching the men of impudence he will say:

The ignorant is upon the throne, the learned outside the door,
Seeking a way by trickery, he can't even reach the doorman.[58]

Concerning fidelity, they say that it is the result of the baseness of the carnal soul and excessive avidity. If someone receives a trivial thing from a patron or a friend, or attains some livelihood from the latter or former, greed and avarice will induce him to seek more, and he will pester that person every day like an impudent leech to such an extent that the poor man will be sick and tired of his life due to the intruder, and he will seek a way to rid himself of the company of such a nuisance.

Seeing the Angel of Death is better than seeing you.[59]

The ancients have unknowingly praised such behavior, and have likened the person who has reached the height of fidelity to a dog. One must rather have in mind his own interest, and when the goal is attained and no expectations are left, he should turn his back on everyone, even his own father. A man should spend every morning

---

58 This poem is by Rashid Watwat (d. 1195 A.D.), quoted in *Akhlaq al-Ashraf*, ed. by Ali Asghar Halabi, Tehran, 1995, p. 191.

59 This line is by Sa'di and the full couplet reads:
    Instead of your touch I prefer the scorpion's bite.
    In truth the Angel of Death is more pleasing to my sight.
(*Kuliyyat* of Sa'di, ed. by Iqbal Ashtiani, p. 18)

and evening in new company. To enjoy life, one should be unrestrained, so that one may fully enjoy the company and wealth of his peers. Consequently, people will not be saddened by him, and will know for certain that:

A morsel from every pot is delightful.

ANECDOTE

It has been related that Muhyy al-Din Arabi,[60] who was the great philosopher and leader of the scholars of his time, for thirty years was intimately associated day and night with Muwlana Nur al-Din Rasadi,[61] and they could not rest one moment without being in each other's company. In the last few days of the life of Nur al-Din, Muhyy al-Din was busy drinking wine at his bedside. After going one night to his own chamber and returning the next morning, he saw that the slaves had cut their hair and were bewailing the death of Nur al-Din. He asked what had happened. They said that Nur al-Din had passed away. Muhyy al-Din said, "Alas! Nur al-Din." Then turning to his slave he said, "Let us go and find another companion," and then he went to his quarters. They say that he lived for twenty years after that incident and that no one heard the name of Nur al-Din from his lips.

In truth, it is only appropriate to our contemporaries to learn fidelity from this unique philosopher of his time. Another obvious proof (of the uselessness of fidelity) is that whoever had persisted in faithfulness will always be dejected and will eventually spend his life in futility, as was the case with Farhad, who carved Mount Bisutun; he never reached his goal, and finally spent his sweet (shirin) life in pursuit of Shirin.[62] While he was dying, he said:

---

60 Muhyy al-Din Mohammad Ibn al-Arabi (1165–1240, the great Sufi of the Islamic world, who was born in Murcia, Spain, lived in various cities of the Middle East, and died in Damascus. He is the author of many works, of which the *Fusus al-Hikam* (Bezels of Philosophy) is the most well known.

61 The editor of *Akhlaq al-Ashraf*, Dr. Hallabi, has found a reference in Dawlatshah Samarqandi's *Tazkerat'ul-Shu'ara* (Mohammad Abbasi edition, p. 184) to this person, but the time of his life does not correspond to the time of Ibn Arabi. His identity is uncertain.

62 Shirin was the niece of the queen of Armenia who became the favorite wife of

The wretched Farhad his sweet life did give
Not knowing that still his Shirin did live.

And that hapless lover who is known as Majnun[63] of Bani `Amir who was at first a wise and learned youth was suddenly struck by the love of a girl called Layli. In faithfulness to her, life became bitter to him, and he could never enjoy her. He would run naked in the deserts and sing:

If along the way Layli and I all alone were to meet
The pilgrimage to Mecca I would make with bare feet.

Our great men are right. People who meet such an end should be avoided. But concerning sincerity they say that it is the worst of attributes because sincerity is the source of loss and animosity. One who is sincere will never prosper. As much as possible a man must flatter his friends and patrons, and lie hypocritically, and make the phrase "The emir says the truth" his motto. He would say whatever pleases people. For instance, if at midnight a great man says, "Now it is the time of the early prayer," one should leap forward saying, "In truth it is." [64] And one should add that today the sun is very

Khosrow Parviz, the Sasanian king. She committed suicide at the grave of Khosrow when he was killed by his son Shiruya. *Khosrow ve Shirin* is one of the famous verse romances of Nezami (1141–1204), in which another man, the stonecutter Farhad, is also in love with Shirin. According to Persian tradition, he carves inscriptions and pictures on Mount Bistun for the sake of her love, and when he is treacherously led to believe by Khosrow that Shirin has died, he kills himself. The couplet that follows is from that work.

63 Layli and Majnun were two famous Arab lovers whose tragic love has become the subject of many poems. The first adaptation of the story in English was by Issac Disraeli in 1799 as The Loves of Majnun and Leila. "Majnun" or "the Distracted Lover" was a nickname for Qais Amiri, to whom an Arabic Divan of poems is attributed. The poem that follows is from it (Divan, Bombay ed. 1901, p. 8).

64 This line is in fact a paraphrase of a story in the *Gulistan*, 1st chapter "On the Manners of Kings" (Furughi ed., p. 47) in which Buzurgmehr, the minister of Anushiravan, is criticized by the king and the dignitaries of the court for expressing his candid opinion. Sa'di mockingly adds:
> *In counsel 'gainst the wish of kings to stand*
> *Is a man's own blood to wash his hand:*
> *If he shall call the broadest daytime night*
> *Say: "Yea, Sire! Moon and planets swim in sight!"*
(Translation by E. Arnold from the *Gulistan*, Harper & Brothers, New York, 1899, p. 72.)

warm, and in order to prove it he should swear by the Qur'an or by an irrevocable divorce of his wife. If an old, miserly and ugly eunuch is being addressed, he should be called "the champion of the age," "the most chaste of the world," "a sweet budding youth," "the Joseph of Egypt," and "the generous Hatam Ta`i" so that one might benefit from his gold, his bounty, his robes of honor and his influence, and thus establish one's friendship in the eunuch's heart. If one calls a hairless man bald, or a hernia a rupture, or a wife-prostituted husband a cuckold, for the sake of this ill-omened truth he will cause displeasure and having the power, the offended party will give him a sound thrashing. And if the cuckold or the bald man is weak, they will cause him trouble in a myriad other ways. Consequently, for the rest of one's life, thanks to having spoken this one word of truth, antagonism will not end between them. This is why great men have said, "Better a lie of good intention than an ugly truth to mention.[65]

What better evidence is there than if a truthful man gives a hundred truthful testimonies, not only will he not be appreciated, but those who hear him will even be annoyed and will bring forth a hundred interpretations to falsify him; but if a faithless man be found willing to give a false testimony they will bribe him in a hundred ways and lavish various kindnesses upon him so that he will give that testimony. It is for the very same reason that today in Islamic countries many thousands of judges, sheikhs, theologians, and reliable witnesses and their dependents earn their livelihood in this way, and they say:

> *A lie which brings you happiness*
> *Is better than a truth that causes sadness.[66]*

Concerning mercy and compassion, our masters have great doubts. They say whoever pities an oppressed or deprived person has sinned and made himself the object of [Divine] wrath. Their argument is that nothing happens without God's desire and knowledge.

---

65 This is a well-known line by Sa'di in the *Gulistan* (1st story of the first chapter) (Furughi ed., pp. 13–14).

66 This is a line by attributed to Sa'di.

Therefore whatever comes to His servants comes out of necessity from His Exalted desire.

Plato says: "The case is not eventuated unless it is necessitated." God, who is the Most Merciful, surely would not have sent misfortune, had that person been unworthy of it, because whatever befalls a person befits that person. As the proverb says:

May the dog be hungry, the raven blind, and the goat lean.

And also it has been said:

There is no blind man unworthy of his blindness.

So if you want to have pity on a person who has been struck by God's wrath, you will sin and be a transgressor, and will be punished on the day of Resurrection for it. An analogy would be when a slave whose master has been beating him in order to train him is told by a stranger, "Your master is doing wrong in beating you. You should be rewarded and given a robe of honor." Clearly, the master will be annoyed by such a person.

ANECDOTE

In the blessed days of the Prophet, the pagans were told to feed the poor. They answered, "The poor are the servants of God. If He wanted to feed them, He would have done so. If He does not, why should we?" Similarly, the Qur'an states: "Are we to feed those whom God would have fed if He chose? Surely you are in manifest error."[67] So it is incumbent upon every created being not to pity and or heed the condition of an oppressed or wounded person, an orphan, a family man in distress or a servant who has grown old and crippled serving in the house of his master. Rather, for the sake of God, he should aggravate them as much as he can, so that his reward and station may be elevated, and on the day of Resurrection,

---

67 Qur'an, 36:47. The actual quotation is this:
And when they are told, "Spend ye of (the bounties) with which God has provided you," the unbelievers say to those who believe: "Shall we then feed those whom, if God had so willed, He would have fed, (Himself)? – Ye are in nothing but manifest error...." This last part, which conveys the true meaning of the verse, is omitted by Obeyd.

when "neither wealth nor children will be of any help,"[68] this will come to his aid.

This was what I had promised at the beginning of the book to my brothers. It is hoped that if a novice persists in emulating the characteristics of great men and makes them part of his rational soul he will succeed both in this world and the next.

---

68 Qur'an, 26:88.

DEFINITIONS

CHAPTER ONE

THE WORLD AND WHAT IS THEREIN

The World: *That in which no creature can rest.*

The Wise Man: *He who does not concern himself with the world and its people.*

The Perfect Man: *He who is not greatly affected by sadness or joy.*

The Generous: *He who does not have his eyes on other people's property.*

The Ideal Man: *He who wishes good for everyone.*

The Man: *He who is no hypocrite.*

Thought: *That which worries people sick for no purpose.*

The Man of Learning: *He who cannot even earn his own livelihood.*

The Ignorant: *Fortune's favorite.*

The Miser: *The wealthy.*

The Failure: *The seeker of learning.*

The Professor: *Chief of all failures.*

His Assistant: *The ever-desirous.*

The Miserable: *The theologian.*

The Well of Disappointment: *His inkwell.*

The Broken: *His pen.*

The Pawned: *His book.*

The Dirty: *His folder.*

The Mother of Sleep: *His studies.*

The Closed One: *His school.*

Wasted and Ruined: *His time.*

The Used Up: *Religious endowments.*

The Administrator of a Trust: *He that carries it with him.*

The Salary, Stipend and Wages: *Things which do not reach
the public.*

The Promissory Note: *A useless piece of paper that worries people.*

The Injunction: *A letter written by a governor to his deputies,
and which they ignore.*

Weak Willed:[1] *The governor whose deputies ignore him.*

SECOND CHAPTER

ON THE TURKS AND THEIR FRIENDS

Gog and Magog: *The Turkish tribes when they invade a country.*

The Infernal Guards: *Their vanguards.*

The Famine: *The result of their invasion.*

The Confiscation and Distribution: *Their gifts.*

The Flag of Calamity: *Their banner.*

Plundering: *Their profession.*

The Sudden Earthquake: *When they come.*

The Angels of Interrogation:[2] *The two heralds who stand guard at
the door leaning on their clubs.*

---

1 The original, *teez reesh*, is a slanderous word that translates as "fart to the beard,"
meaning "old fart."

2 According to Islamic tradition, two angels, Nakir and Munkar, interrogate the dead.

Canis Major: *Night watchman.*

Canis Minor: *His deputy*

The Plunderer: *The envoy.*

The Hay of Hell: *The fodder of their horses.*

The Hot Water of Hell: *Their wine.*

The Unjust: *The officer for the endowment.*

The One Who Should be Killed:[3] *The holder of the seal of the city.*

The Foreman: *The thief.*

The Jackal: *The secretary of the Chancellery.*

The General: *The thief of the warehouse.*

The Constable: *He who robs by night and asks the shopkeeper for his wages by day.*

The Tax Collector: *He who puts the squeeze on the thief.*

THIRD CHAPTER

ON THE JUDGE AND HIS FOLLOWERS

The Judge: *He who is cursed by everyone.*

The Cottonball: *His turban.*

His Deputy: *The faithless.*

The Attorney-at-law: *He who distorts the truth.*

Justice: *That which never speaks the truth.*

The Meditator: *He with whom neither man nor God is pleased.*

The Judge's Retinue: *Those whose testimony is an interest-free loan.*

The Importunate: *His servant.*

The Ill-Omened: *His friends.*

The Seeker of Gold: *His Companion.*

Heaven: *What they will never see.*

---

3 *Tamqachi* was an official in possession of the tax collector's seal.

Lawful Money: *What they never want.*

The Properties of Orphans
and Endowments: *What they regard as their own.*

The Eye of the Judge: *A vessel that never fills.*

Dreadful: *His end.*

The Bottom of Hell: *His place.*

The House of Fire: *His courtroom.*

Satan's Threshold: *Its threshold.*

The River of Fire, the Scorching Desert,
the Bottomless Pit and the River of Woes: *Its four corners.*

Bribery: *The helper of the helpless.*

The Lucky: *One who does not see the face of the judge.*

The Drunken Carousel: *A place frequented by the judge.*

The Preacher: *An ass.*

The Prelector: *The tail of an ass.*

The Clergyman: *One who preaches but does not practice.*

The Teacher: *The fool.*

The Courtier: *A sycophant.*

The Fox: *A clergyman that always accompanies the emirs and khans.*

The Poet: *A greedy braggart.*

FOURTH CHAPTER

ON SHEIKHS AND THEIR DEPENDENTS

The Sheikh: *The devil himself.*

The Donkey: *His son.*

The Devils: *His followers.*

Hypocrisy: *What he says about the world.*

Nonsense: *What he says about the world to come.*

Delirium: *His dreams.*

The Sufi: *A freeloader.*

The Hajji: *He who swears falsely by the Ka'ba.*

The Pilgrim of Two Holy Places:[4] *May God increase the torture of that accursed devil.*

FIFTH CHAPTER

ON THE GENTRY AND THEIR MANNERS

Boasting and Insolence: *The stock-in-trade of the gentry.*

Nothing: *Their existence.*

Hollow: *Their courtesies.*

Vanity and Folly: *Their talk.*

Disapproval, Greed, Malice and Envy: *Their characteristics.*

The Fool: *He who expects any good from them.*

The Wretched and Unfortunate: *Their attendants.*

What is Lost: *Their generosity.*

Non-existent: *Their good behavior.*

The Phoenix of the West:[5] *Justice and humanity.*

Roguery, Violence, Hypocrisy, Dissimulation and Falsehood: *The ways of the great men.*

Lust: *Their main ailment.*

---

4 The two holy places are Mecca and Medina, and whoever visits them is called Hajji al-Haramayn.

5 The Phoenix of the West (*Anqa-i-Maghreb*) is a legendary bird and thus, non-existent.

SIXTH CHAPTER

ON ARTISANS AND OFFICIALS

The Businessman: *He who fears not God.*

The Cloth-merchant: *The highwayman.*

The Money-changer: *The petty thief.*

The Tailor: *The nimble-handed one.*

The Imam: *The seller of prayers.*

The Druggist: *He who wishes everyone sick.*

The Forger: *The goldsmith.*

The Physician: *The executioner.*

The Liar: *The astronomer.*

The Unfortunate: *The fortuneteller.*

The Wrestler: *The idle rogue.*

The Bath-attendant: *The key-holder to coitus.*

The Salesman: *The brigand of the market.*

SEVENTH CHAPTER

ON WINE AND MATTERS PERTAINING TO IT.

Wine: *The cause of every trouble.*

Backgammon, the Cup-bearer,
   the Candle and Sweetmeats: *Its means.*

The Harp, the Lute, the Flute: *Its instruments.*

Soup and Kebab: *Its food.*

The Meadow and Garden: *Its place.*

Poison: *The early morning wine.*

The Free: *The drunk.*

The Carefree: *The Tipsy.*

The Angel of Death: *A bearded saghi.*

The Conjunction of
    Two Evil Stars: *Two bearded saghis kissing each other.*

The Alert: *The sober amongst the drunk.*

The Laughing Stock: *The drunk amongst the sober.*

Brawling: *A prayer performed in the tavern.*

The Destroyer of Joys: *Ramadan.*

The "Hallowed Night":[6] *The festival ending that month.*

Satan, the Ill-Wisher
    and the Meddler: *He who sits next to you in the chess or back-*
                    gammon game and instructs your opponents.

Heaven: *Company of the beloved.*

Calamity: *Meeting of the rival.*

EIGHTH CHAPTER

ON BHANG AND ITS ACCESSORIES

Bhang: *That which fills the Sufi with ecstasy.*

Chess: *Its means.*

The Lute and the Tambourine: *Its instruments.*

A Sunny Corner: *Its place.*

A Dish of Meat and Rice accompanied with Sweetmeats: *Its food.*

The Woolen Cloak and Camelhair Poncho: *His clothes.*

Nobility on Both Sides: *He who takes bhang with wine.*

The Deprived: *He who does not do so.*

---

6 This was the night in which the Qur'an was revealed to the Prophet Mohammad.

THE HOUSEHOLDER AND THE THINGS PERTAINING TO HIM

OBEYD-E
ZAKANI

The Bachelor: *He who enjoys the world.*

The Ghoul: *The procuress.*

The Unfortunate: *The householder.*

The Two-horned:[7] *He who has two wives.*

The Most Unfortunate of the Unfortunates: *He who has more.*

The Sour-faced Cuckold: *The father-in-law.*

The Cold-hearted Shrew: *The mother-in-law.*

The Futile: *The householder's life.*

Wasted: *His time.*

Dissipated: *His wealth.*

Distracted: *His mind.*

Bitter: *His enjoyment.*

The Abode of Mourning: *His house.*

The Family Foe: *His son.*

The Unlucky: *A young man with an old wife.*

The Cuckold: *An old man with a young wife.*

The Horned Ram: *A man whose wife reads the romance of Vis and Ramin*[8]**Divorce:** *His Cure.*

Joy after Sorrow:[9] *The triple divorce.*

Love: *The occupation of the idle ones.*

---

7 Zul Qarnain (a man with two horns) is supposed to be either Alexander or Cyrus the Great. In surah 18:83-98 the name apparently comes from the shape of his helmet – a man with two horns. Having two horns represents a terrible affliction. Obeyd equates such a condition with having two wives.

8 For *Vis va Ramin* see note 8 of "One Hundred Maxims".

9 *Al-Faraj Ba'd al-Shidda* (Joy after Sorrow) is in fact the name of a work in Arabic by Muhsin al-Tanukhi. It was rendered into Persian by Mohammad Aufi, and then made into another collection of stories under the same name by Husain Mu'ayyid Dehistani.

ON THE TRUE NATURE OF MEN AND WOMEN

The Lady: *She who has many lovers.*

The Housewife: *She who has a few.*

The Virtuous: *She who is content with one lover.*

The Real Lady: *She who makes love gratis.*

The Charitable: *A man who makes love to an old lady.*

The Poor: *She who is after strangers.*

The Aphrodisiac: *The leg of another's wife.*

Virginity: *A name denoting nothing.*

THE TREATISE OF ONE HUNDRED MAXIMS

I would like to present to the thoughtful and sagacious reader the fact that the present writer, Obeyd-e Zakani, may God fulfill his desires, though he has no high standing in the world of learning, nonetheless has devoted himself since his youth to pursuing knowledge and reading books and attending the lectures of the learned and the philosophers. It so happened that in the year 750 A.H. (1350 CE) a work of Plato, the prince of philosophers, written for the sake of his pupil Aristotle and translated from the Greek into Persian by the unrivalled man of our times, Nasir al-Din Tusi,[1] fell into my hands. This work on ethics was accompanied by some other treatises such as *The Book of the Counsels* of the just king Anushiravan,[2] which was dictated to Taj Rabi.[3] After reading these with much eagerness

---

1 Nasir al-Din Tusi (1201–1274) was a great philosopher, astronomer, mathematician and statesman. He was first in the service of the Isma'ilis of Alamut, and after Hulagu defeated them in 1256 Nasir al-Din offered him his services. Nasir al-Din rewrote many scientific and philosophical works that had been translated from Greek into Arabic and Persian, but unlike what Obeyd-e Zakani claims, he does not seem to have known Greek himself. The works of Tusi entitled *Al-awsaf al-Ashraf* (Descriptions of noblemen) and *Akhlaq-i Nasiri* (Nasirian ethics) seem to have been special objects of satire for Obeyd. In the *Nasirian Ethics* (trans. by G. M. Wickens, London, 1964, pp. 258–60), Tusi gives a number of maxims or "testaments" attributed to Plato and which seem to have inspired Obeyd.

2 See note 6 to Chapter 4.

3 Anushiravan displayed a great interest in learning and literature. It was during his reign that the celebrated book *Kalileh va Dimneh* as well as the game of chess were brought from India. Among didactical works of his reign is a collection of maxims attributed to his minister Buzorgmehr. However, I could not find any reference to Taj Rabi'. Apart from Buzorgmehr's book, there is a versified version of Anushiravan's *Counsels*, which probably was written by a Persian poet in the late eleventh century. The poet's name is given as Sharif or Badaye'i (see Charles Scheffer, *Chrestomathie Persane*, Paris, 1883, pp. 205–32; Said Nafisi, "Pand Nameh-ye Anushiravan," *Mehr*, nos. 2–3, 1934, pp. 181–88 and 254–64). Interestingly enough some maxims in this book somewhat correspond to what we find in the "One Hundred Maxims" of Obeyd.

and enthusiasm, the author decided to compose a book of counsels in a similar fashion, which would be a work of sincerity, devoid of the shadow of hypocrisy and signs of affectation – a kind of book that will be beneficial to everyone and also will enable the writer to be ranked among the men of taste. It is hoped that everyone will profit greatly from these pieces of advice.

If you need a medicinal draught,
Then by my counsel's cure be taught,
In wisdom's sieve it is sifted through
And mixed with wit's sweet honey, too.

1. O dear friends, make the most of your life.

2. Do not waste your time.

3. Do not leave the pleasures of today for tomorrow.

4. Do not spoil a good day.

5. Consider wealth, leisure and health as a real kingdom.

6. Enjoy the present, since you will not live a second life.

7. If someone forgets his origin and status, do not remind him of them.

8. Do not greet the conceited.

9. Do not count the days of illness among the days of your life.

10. Give our regards to the high-spirited and good-natured people of dervish-like temperament.

Here are some examples: "Do not lodge near the palace of the king"; "Do not expect fidelity of gossip-mongers"; "Do not become a captive in the hands of women"; "Do not expect any good of young women when you become old."

11.   Forget about expecting help from other people, so that you merrily can laugh in their faces.

12.   Do not frequent the courts of the kings, and forsake their rewards in order to avoid their chamberlains.[4]

13.   Sacrifice even your life for the sake of good friends.

14.   Consider seeing beautiful people as the happiness of life, the light of the eye and the joy of the heart.

15.   Curse those who lift their eyebrows, wrinkle their foreheads, talk seriously and have a sour face, as well those who are ill-tempered, liars, miserly and ill-mannered.

16.   Pass wind onto the beards[5] of merciless lords and dignitaries.

17.   As much as possible refrain from speaking the truth, so that you may not become a bore to other people, and cause undue annoyance.

18.   Engage in ribaldry, cuckoldry, gossip, ingratitude, false testimony, selling heaven for the world, and playing the tambourine, so that you may become dear to the great and enjoy your life.

19.   Don't believe the sermons of the clerics, lest you go astray and end up in hell.

20.   If you want salvation, attach yourself to the service of the all-sacrificing and pure-hearted rends[6] in order to be saved.

---

4 The *hajib,* chamberlain or usher, was an important official in the court of Iranian kings, and one had to see him before being admitted to an audience.

5 Literally, "To fart in the beard of someone" means "to hell with someone" or "to ignore him completely."

6 The terms *rend* and *qalandar* as explained in the introduction, are difficult to translate because of their rich cultural associations. Apparently, both words originally meant something like a "rogue" or "scoundrel" and were probably used in official circles to describe the people who deviated from the norm and were considered social rebels. Gradually these terms, especially in Sufi terminology, came to have meanings such as "devil of a fellow," "initiate," or even the "perfect man." On the subject of *rend*, see J. C. Brugel's article entitled "Pious Rogue" in *Edebiya*t, vol. 4, no. 1, 1979, pp. 43–64.

21.   Do not take lodging in the neighborhood of the sanctimonious clerics, so that you may live to your heart's delight.

22.   Do not take rooms in a street where there is a minaret, so that you may be safe from the annoyance of cacophonous muezzins.

23.   Help the addict by giving him food and sweetmeats.

24.   Give a helping hand to the drunkards.

25.   As long as you live, live happily without a thought for your heirs.

26.   Consider being a bachelor and a qalandar[7] as the foundation of a life of happiness.

27.   Liberate yourself from the chains of good and ill repute, so that you may live freely.

28.   Don't fall into the traps of women, especially widows with brats.

---

7 While having similar connotations as *rend*, *qalandar* is used for a dervish who does not care about his clothes and appearance, nor about the hypocritical manners and customs of society. In the age of Obeyd-e Zakani the term was used for the members of a Malamati Sufi order. On this subject see the introduction of the present volume; see also Ahmad Ali Raja'i, *Farhang-i Ash'ar-i Hafez*, Tehran, 1951, pp. 492–96; E. G. Browne, *A Year Amongst the Persians*, Cambridge, 1927, pp. 531–89; Helmut Ritter, *Das Mer der Seele, Welt and Gott in den Geschichten des Farid al-Din Attar*, Leiden, 1978, pp. 487–91; and *Khatib-i Farsi, Manakib-i Camal al-Din Savi*, ed. by Tahsin Yazici, Ankara, 1972.

A recent book by Mohammad Reza Shafi'i Kadkani, *Qalandariye dar Tarikh: Degardisiha-ye Yek Ideology*, Sokhan Publications: Tehran, 2007, has given an interesting and in-depth study of *galandariye* in Iranian history.

In the collected works of Obeyd, there are two letters where he pokes fun at the *qalandars*. These letters are interesting because of his usage of the terminology of the *qalanadariye* order, such as "langar" (literally meaning "anchor," was a gathering place for *qalandars*) and "takiyeh (a Sufi monastery). In some of his poems, his attitude towards the *qalandars* is very positive (*Kulliyat*, p. 263).

29. Do not waste your precious time on lawful but cold love-making.

30. Do not marry daughters of judges, theologians, sheikhs or dignitaries, and if such a union does take place against your will, have anal intercourse with your bride lest her evil origin show itself and your children become hypocrites, beggars or headaches for their parents.

31. Don't marry the daughter of a preacher, lest she give birth to an ass.

32. Fear the provision for the wet-nurse, the philosophizing of the midwife, the dominance of the pregnant wife, the babble of the cradle, the greeting of the son-in-law, the duties toward the wife, and the commotion of the child.

33. Consider masturbation far better than seduction.

34. Don't expect the friendship of young women when you become old.

35. Don't make love to old women gratis.

36. Don't get married, lest you become a pimp.

A group of qalandars are we, strangers to hypocrisy.
Deception, pomp, and duplicity are not our ideology.
To none are we known as a friend in any terrain.
In no town can any our acquaintance claim.
If unknown be our name, then unknown let us be,
If we have nothing, then of all let us be free.
The dazed amongst us you won't see seeking gold,
The crazed amongst us you won't see with garden or abode.
In the langar where we are, grief is foreign company,
In the takieh where we sit, there is only sincerity.
We fear not the policeman or market constable
For he who has submitted is fearless of worldly trouble
If the flower be far from reach, then with a thorn are we pleased,
And if there be no straw mat, then on the dust we are at ease.
Each in every group has his hope somewhere sown,
We have chosen God as the place of our hope alone.
Like Obeyd in begging we do not see any shame,
In the Qalandariye, Sufi is not a beggar's name.

37. Beat old women soundly in order to attain the status of the warriors for the Faith.

38. On the street, don't be deceived either by the tall stature of veiled women or by the veils hemmed with brocade.

39. Take advantage of the money and bodies of slaves, so that you may be regarded as a perfectly law-abiding man.

40. Don't leave idle the instruments of eating and copulating for a moment.

41. Whenever you find pretty boys drunk and asleep, seize the opportunity before they wake up.

42. Extend the alms of your sexual favors to such deserving persons as secluded women who cannot leave their houses, old and penniless homosexuals, youths whose beards have grown and prevent them from doing their business, and young women whose husbands have gone on a trip, since giving alms brings great blessings.

43. Do not wine and dine alone, since this is the practice of the Jews and judges.

44. Do not ask anything of the upstart sons of beggars.

45. Buy Turkish slave boys at any price when they have no beard, and sell them at any price when their beards begin to grow.

46. Do not withhold your posterior favors from friends and foes when young so that in old age you can attain the status of a sheikh, a preacher or a man of fame and dignity.

47. Buy soft-handed, not hard-fisted, slaves.

48. Do not take wine from the hand of a bearded Saki.

49. Do not expect comfort, peace and blessing in the house of a man with two wives.

50. Expect neither chastity from a lady who reads the romance of *Vis and Ramin*[8] nor anal integrity from a boy who drinks wine and smokes bhang.

51. Have anal intercourse with the daughter of your neighbor and do not tamper with her hymen so that you will not have betrayed your neighbor's trust and you will have been a considerate and good Moslem. Thus on her wedding night she will not be ashamed before the bridegroom and she will be proud among the people.

52. In this age of ours do not expect to find a just governor, a judge who does not accept bribes, an ascetic who does not speak hypocritically, a pious chamberlain, or a statesman who has preserved his anal integrity.

53. If you want God to be compassionate to you, show compassion toward young women whose husbands have gone on a trip, toward the lover who has a chance with his beloved for the first time but fails to perform, toward a cupbearer who goes to a party where a rake does not like him and turns him out, toward a group of half drunk men who have spilt their wine, toward the young man in the hands of a shrewish wife, and toward the girl who has lost her virginity and fears the approaching wedding night.

54. Have intercourse with women on their death bed as much as possible and consider this a great opportunity.

55. With children be content with a dry humping so that you will have been kind toward them.

---

8 *Vis va Ramin* is a romance by Fakhraddin Gorgani (11th century). Since the story is taken from a pre-Islamic source, it tells of the passionate love of Vis for her brother Viru, to whom she is betrothed before she falls in love with Ramin. It seems that this romance has had a reputation for licentiousness and eroticism during the Islamic period. For an account of this work see V. Minorsky, *Bist-maqala* (A Memorial Volume), London, 1964, "*Vis-u-Ramin*, a Parthian Romance," pp. 151–99. For a complete English verse translation of *Vis va Ramin* see *Vis and Ramin* translated by Dick Davis, Mage Publishers, 2008.

56. Do not consider the man who floors his opponent an athlete or a wrestler, but rather the one who places his face on the floor and eagerly lets the other one mount him.

57. Don't pin your hopes upon the promise of the drunk, coquetry of women, vow of hookers, and the compliments of homosexuals.

58. Be courteous to your teachers, masters, patrons and bed partners, so that you will not be betrayed.

59. Do not be offended by the cursing of beggars, the slapping of women, and the sayings of poets and jesters.

60. Enjoy sleeping with handsome boys because it is a joy that you will not find in heaven.

61. Exercise every trick that you know in gambling and backgammon so that you might be called a perfect gambler. If the other party presses you hard, vow that if you are not speaking the truth may your wife be divorced irrevocably,[9] because swearing is not a sin in gambling.

62. Do not pay young boys and prostitutes before finishing with them so that they will not deny it in the end and so there won't be a fuss.

63. Do not let talkative, gossipy and mean people into your parties nor drunkards and inharmonious minstrels who repeat their doleful songs endlessly.

64. Keep away from a party of brawlers.

65. Do not lodge a prostitute and a pretty boy in the same room.

66. Do not play backgammon on credit so that you will not talk people's heads off in vain.

---

9 In Islam if a man declares three times that he has divorced his wife, he can not return to her unless she marries another man and then gets divorced. *Se talaqeh-kardan*, or divorcing one's wife three times, also can be used as a kind of oath.

67. Be cautious when you take a young boy to your room and when he leaves be on your guard that he does not steal something from you.

68. Unless you see food and sweetmeats laid before you, do not start smoking bhang.

69. Tell the busy-bodies and revelers with hung-overs to go to hell when in the morning they frown at you and blame and criticize you, saying that the night before you were badly drunk, broke the bottle and gave away your money and clothes, so that they won't bother the others as well.

70. Beat women hard and then make love to them passionately so that they will fear and obey you. The work of the master of the house can be achieved through fear and hope, and displeasure changes to pleasantness.

71. With compliments and sweet words seduce your beloved.

72. Do not go drunk near a pond or a stream so that you may not fall in.

73. Do not talk with sheikhs, the newly rich, fortune tellers, morticians, mendicants,[10] chess players, spendthrifts, descendants of old families or any others stricken with misfortune.

74. Do not expect honesty, fairness and the conduct befitting a good Moslem from a businessman.

75. Do not grudge gentle slapping and robbing from old homosexuals.

76. Beware of the hypocrisy of judges, the uproar of the Mongols, the hue and cry of pederasts, and the friendship of those with whom you once had an affair and who are now daring and powerful men. Beware also of the tongues of

---

10 A *kongar-zan* was a special kind of beggar who would beat a horn and a comb together and ask for money. If he failed to get money he sometimes would threaten to inflict a wound upon himself.

poets, the deception of women, the evil eyes of jealous people and the hatred of your relatives.

77. Do not expect anything of a disobedient child, a shrewish wife, an old and crazy horse, a servant who wants to nail you down, or a useless friend.

78. Do not pass wind without a proper ablution at the foot of the preacher's pulpit, because it has not been authorized by past scholars.

79. Consider youth better than old age, health better than illness, wealth better than poverty, prostitution better than cuckoldry, drunkenness better than soberness, and wisdom better than madness.

80. Do not repent lest you become unfortunate, ill-starred, afflicted and boring.

81. Do not go on the pilgrimage of the Hajj lest greed overcomes you and you become faithless and unjust.

82. Do not show the house of your beloved to anyone.

83. Do not make love to women alone because such is not gentlemanly.

84. Do not be ashamed of cuckoldry so that you can spend your days without sorrow and your nights without any thought.

85. Be friends with wine sellers and traffickers in bhang so that you will insure your future pleasures.

86. Do not drink wine in front of people in the fasting month of Ramadan so that they will not look at you as an apostate.

87. Do not accept the testimony of the blind in the month of Ramadan even if they be on a mountain top.

88. Do not ask the poll tax of shoe-makers, cuppers, and weavers if they are Moslems.

89. Do not exaggerate being honest and faithful, lest you become afflicted with colic or other such ailments.

90. Make a point to attend early morning bhang and wine parties so that fortune may come to you, for corruption has great auspiciousness everywhere.

91. Try to lie with the sons of the sheikhs by whatever means because this is considered a virtue comparable to a great pilgrimage.

92. Do not make yourself known as a generous man in the tavern, the gambling hall, or the parties of hookers and pederasts so that they will not turn to you for everything.

93. Do not offer your place to the nouveau riche or to the upstart sons of slaves and peasants.

94. Flee from indebtedness to your relatives, from the table of the miserly, from the grimace of servants, from the discord of your family members, and from those who ask for loans.

95. At any rate, avoid death because it has been disliked since the days of old.

96. Do not throw yourself into a well and injure yourself unless absolutely necessary.

97. Do not listen to the words of sheikhs and opium smokers since it has been said:

> *Whatever piece of wisdom a smoker of opium imparts,*
> *Write it on the phallus of an ass and offer it to him.*

98. Sow your seed unlawfully so that your children will become theologians, sheikhs and favorites of the king.

99. Despise not ribaldry, nor look down at satirists.

100. Take heed and listen to these words willingly, as they are the words of great men

These are the sayings that have reached us from our masters and from great men. We have also mentioned in this brief account our gleanings from books and our observations from the biographies of great men, so that those ready and well disposed might benefit from them:

> *Fortunate ones take heed of advice*
>
> *Great men accept the counsel of dervishes.*[11]

May God Almighty open the door of happiness, peace and strength to all.

---

11 This poem is from Sa'di.

PREFACE TO THE JOYOUS TREATISE
Hasan Javadi

Before going to Obeyd-e Zakani's stories and anecdotes *(Resaleh-ye Delgosha* – The Joyous Treatise), I would like to give a general view of the historical and popular characters that appear in them and compare some of these stories with other sources. One interesting point to note is that nearly all the Arabic stories relate to an earlier period and are about such Umayyad and Abbasid caliphs as Mu'awiyya, Yazid, Mahdi, Harun al-Rashid, Ma'mun, Mutawakkil and Watheq, and such characters as the minister Ja'far Barmacide, the poet Abu Nuwas, the muscian Ishaq of Mosul and the scholar and writer Jahiz. In contrast, the Persian stories of the *Risaleh-ye Delgosha* predominantly relate to more contemporary figures such as the Atabek Sulgar Shah (first part of the 13th century), the Mongol emir Tugachar (d. 1295), the minister Shams al-Din Sahib Divan (d. 1284) and his son Baha al-Din (d.1279), the well-known vizier Rashid al-Din Fadl-allah (d. 1318) and his son Giyath al-Din (d. 1336), Sultan Abu Said (d. 1335), and a number of other poets, theologians and scholars of this period. It seems that the Arabic stories (93 in number) are mostly derived from various Arabic joke books or *Nawader* books and relate to the earlier period of Islamic history, whereas the Persian stories (226 in number), with the exception of a few, are about characters nearer to Obeyd's own time. Of the latter group, seven relate to the Umayyad or Abbasid periods and seventeen to the reign of Sultan Mahmud of Ghazna (d. 1030). Obviously, the stories about Mahmud and his jester Talhak as well as other Persian stories of an earlier period were not likely to be found in Arabic joke books, and they were collected by Obeyd himself.

The characters most often met with in the stories of Obeyd are described below:

JUHA

Juha (sometimes written as Juhi or Joha) is the hero of a great number of popular stories in the Middle East and his popularity extends as far as the Balkans. Most of the jokes attributed to him by the Arabs are attributed by the Turks and the Iranians to Nasr al-Din Hoca (Mulla Nasr al-Din), who was allegedly the jester of Timur-i Lang and died sometime in the fifteenth century in Aq Shahar, Turkey. Most of the parts of the Arabic text, *Nawader of Juha*, which has been published many times in Arab countries, correspond to Persian and Turkish works about Mulla Nasr al-Din. (A comprehensive study of the stories related to Juha has recently been published in Tehran by Ahmad Mujahid, entitled *Juhi*, Tehran University Publications, 2003).

Arthur Christensen in his article "Juhi in Persian Literature" (in *A Volume of Oriental Studies presented to Prof. E. G. Browne*, 1922, pp. 122 *et seq.*) shows that Juha, or Juhi as he sometimes is called in Persian, was a historical personality. The first reference to him comes in the *Kitab al-Mahasin* by Ibrahim al-Baihaqi (10th century) and later in the *Amthal of al-Maidani* (1124). (See also Martin Hartmann, "Schwanke und Schnurren im Islamischen Orient," *Zeitscher d. Vereins f. Volkskunde*, V, p. 50). Furthermore, there are three references by Jalal al-Din Rumi in his work, *Mathnavi*. Apart from the Juhi stories of Obeyd-e Zakani, Christensen has collected nine stories which are from sources earlier than the fifteenth century. Two of these, one related by Al-Maidani and one by Rumi, are also found in the collections of Mulla Nasr al-Din. Christensen therefore concludes that the collection of Nasr al-Din Hoca, more than being a translation of the old joke book, which is mentioned by Ibn Nadim (d. 996) in his *al-Fihrist*, is an independent collection incorporating many of the old stories. Furthermore, the Arabic versions of the *Nawader of Juha* are mostly based on the Turkish collection.

Altogether there are ten stories (one Arabic and nine Persian) among the anecdotes of Obeyd on Juha in Parviz Atabaki's edition

(Tehran, 1963): No. 10 in Arabic (no. 4 in my translation) and nos. 14, 20, 21, 33, 55, 76, 207, 210, and 229, of which only four are translated in the present volume (nos. 9, 11, 12 and 99 of my translations). Two more, nos. 228 and 262 (nos. 107 and 116 in my translation), are given under the name of Juha by Rumi in his *Mathnavi*, but Obeyd does not mention his name in these stories. Furthermore, Christensen has 27 other stories of Obeyd which, although not attributed to Juha, are nonetheless found in the collections of Hoca Nasr al-Din or the *Nawader of Juha* (see "Remarques sur les faceties du *'Ubaid-i-Zakani, avec des extraits de la Risala-ye dilgusha*" in *Acta Orientalia*).

TALHAK AND OTHER JESTERS

Talhak (also written as Talkhak) is perhaps the most frequently mentioned jester in the works of Obeyd. There are thirteen stories about him (and nos. 1, 11, 17, 156, 161, 165, 177, 183, 191, 203, 204, 226 and 105 of the original text are translated). Talhak was a very outspoken and bold character, and apparently in Persian his name has given rise to the word *dalgak* to signify jester. Some Talhak stories are also found among the anecdotes attributed to the court jester of Naser al-Din Shah (1848–1896) who was called Karim Shira'i. For instance, no. 204 (92 in this translation) is identical with a story in which Karim Shira'i receives a donkey saddle as a royal present. This story was later made into a comedy (see Husain Nurbakhsh, *Karim Shira'i Dalqak-e Mashhur-e Darbar-e Naser al-Din Shah*, Tehran, 1958, pp. 396–414). There are also a number of lesser known jesters and wits of old who will be cited individually in the following notes.

Apart from these there are numerous anecdotes about the kings, emirs, poets, theologians and men of letters, who were mostly contemporaries with, or who lived shortly before, Obeyd. In his *Resaleh-ye Delgosha*, as well as in his other satirical works, Obeyd is very candid and revealing about the social mores and degraded morality of people in those turbulent years during the Mongol domination. Abbas Iqbal, the great historian of this period and Obeyd's editor, writes: "By reading the *Resaleh-ye Delgosha* it becomes clear that in the lifetime of Obeyd, or forty or fifty years before him, a number of wise men and scholars, though unique in their knowledge and proficiency in their subjects, when they encountered the social conditions and the tyranny of the rulers, wanted to laugh stoically at everyone and everything. It was through satire and humor that they leveled their criticism at the mighty of the age" (*Kulliyat-e-Obeyd-e Zakani*, p.22). Among these were the celebrated scientist and philosopher Qotb al-Din Shirazi (d. 1310), the well-known writer and philosopher Azud at-Din Iji (d. 1355), the author of the book called *al-Mawaqif* (1335), the poet Majd al-Din Hamgar (d. 1279) and two lesser men of learning, Sharaf al-Din Damghani and Sharaf al-Din Dargazini. As a member this group, Obeyd not only criticized the wrongdoings, depravity and corruption of his age, but also recorded for posterity the biting and witty remarks of these men.

THE JOYOUS TREATISE
RESALEH-YE DELGOSHA

God be praised for His blessings, bounty, benevolence and grace. Similarly praise be upon Mohammad and his family.

To continue: The author of this treatise, Obeyd-e Zakani, may God Almighty fulfill his wishes, says that the virtue of speech, which distinguishes mankind from other animals, has two forms: serious and humorous, and the advantage of the latter to the former is obvious. However, continuous seriousness creates boredom and continuous humor brings forth lightness and lack of dignity. The men of old have said:

> *Seriousness all year round wastes one's life and days*
> *Daily merriment fritters one's dignity away*

But humor is acceptable if it is for the sake of dispelling sorrows and gladdening the heart, as the wise men said: "Humor in speech is like salt in food." Likewise, a poet has said:

> *Console with wine, cure with humor*
> *Your grief-stricken heart;*
> *But take care of the measure*
> *As you would do with salt.*

One should devote some time to studying varieties of humor, and follow the saying of the poet who wrote:

> *Although the Unity of God and explanations of the*
>   *Qur'an are primary,*
> *There should exist delirium and lightness to some degree.*

The reader should excuse me because our great men have thought it permissible to this extent. Following this introduction I thought of some anecdotes and witty remarks, and collected them under two headings: Arabic Anecdotes and Persian Anecdotes. I have called them collectively "The Joyous Treatise" *(Resaleh-ye Dilgosha)* since a delighted heart and a joyous mind are suited for these pages. May God grant us both blessings.

STORIES FROM THE ARABIC

1

A man was asked, "How is it that your son does not resemble you?"
He said, "If the neighbors would leave us alone, our children would
resemble us."

2

A Jew asked a Christian, "Moses or Jesus, which was superior?" He
answered, "Jesus gave life to the dead, but one day Moses quarreled
with a man and threw him to the ground, whereupon the man died.
Jesus spoke while in the cradle, whereas the forty-year-old Moses
would say, O God, loosen the knot in my tongue so that people will
understand me.'"[1]

3

A soldier was asked, "Why don't you want to go to war?" He replied,
"By God, I don't know a single person among the enemy army, and
they don't know me, so how could enmity exist between us?"

4

One day Juha[2] was going to the market to buy a donkey, and a man
asked him, "Where are you heading?" He said, "To the market to
buy a donkey." The man said, "Say *inshallah* (God willing)." Juha
answered, "There is no need for *inshallah*. The donkey is in the mar-
ket and the gold in my pocket." When he reached the market he was
robbed of his gold. Coming back he saw the same man, who asked

---

1 For Jesus see Qur'an 3, 49; 20, 40; and 28, 15; and for Moses see Qur'an 20, 27; 19,
    29–33; and 73, 52.

2 For Juha see page 86.

91

Juha, "Where are you coming from?" He said, "From the market *inshallah*. They stole my money *inshallah*. I could not buy a donkey *inshallah*, and I am going home penniless *inshallah*!"

5

Mu'awiyya[3] was well known for his tolerance, and nobody could anger him. A man claiming that he was capable of it went to see him and said, "I want to marry your mother since she has big buttocks." Mu'awiya replied, "This was the reason for my father's love for her."

6

A slave girl was asked, "Are you a virgin?" She said, "May God forgive my sins, I was."

7

A man saw another man making love to his slave. He asked her, "Why did you do that?" She said, "O master, he swore by your head to make love to me, and you know my love to you. I could not refuse him!"

8

A woman called her husband a penniless pimp. The husband said, "God be praised that none of it is my fault. The former comes from God and the latter from you!"

9

In the month of Ramazan a homosexual boy was asked if business was sluggish. He said, "Yes. But may God keep Christians and Jews for us!"

10

A judge told his people, "Give thanks to God." They thanked God, but asked him, "What was this thanking for?" He said, "We should

---

3 Mu'awiya ibn Abi Sufyan, the first Umayyed caliph who died in 668.

thank God that angels have no excrement, otherwise all our clothes would have been soiled."

11

A young wife went to the judge and complained, "I am a young woman and my husband does not serve me right." The husband said, "I serve her as much as I can." She said, "I am not content with less than five times a night." He said, "More than three times is not in my power." The judge said, "What a strange plight I am in! They don't bring a case to me unless I have to contribute something myself. But, let it be. I will undertake the other two times myself."

12

A man saw a friend who was traveling on a slow-paced donkey, and asked him, "Where are you heading?" He said, "I am going to the Friday prayer." The man retorted, "But today is Tuesday." The friend said, "I would be happy if this donkey gets me to the mosque by Saturday!"

13

A fox was asked, "In escaping from a dog how many tricks do you know?" "More than a hundred, but the best is that the two of us never meet."

14

Abu Dulaf[4] became a Shiite and used to say that whoever was not a Shiite was a bastard. His son told him, "I am not of this sect." Abu Dulaf answered, "Yes, indeed, before I bought your mother I slept with her."

15

A man said to a woman, "I want to taste you to see if you are sweeter than my wife." She said, "Go ask my husband, who has tasted both of us."

---

4 Abu Dulaf. He seems to be one of the early Arab humorists.

Abu Nuwas[5] saw a drunken man and looked at him in amazement and laughed. He was asked, "Why are you laughing, you do the same everyday?" He said, "I had never seen a drunken man before." They said, "How is this possible?" He answered, "I get drunk before everyone and become sober after everyone, so I don't really know how a drunken man behaves."

17

Abu Nuwas was seen sitting one day with a cup of wine in his hand. On his right there were some grapes and on his left some raisins. For every sip he ate one grape and then one raisin. They asked, "What's all this?" He said, "The Father, the Son and the Holy Spirit."

18

A man was complaining about his wife to Abu'l-Ayna.[6] Abu'l-Ana said, "Do you wish her dead?" The man replied, "No, not really." Abu'l-'Ana said, "But how is that you don't if you are so troubled by her?" The man answered, "If I heard the news of her death, I am afraid that I might die of joy!"

19

Abi Harith[7] was asked, "Is it possible for an eighty-year-old man to have a child?" He said, "Yes, provided he has a twenty-year-old neighbor."

5　Abu Nuwas (d. circa 810 CE), who is remembered through the *Arabian Nights* as the hero of countless droll adventures and facetious stories, was also a great poet. In fact, according to some critics, he ranks above all his contemporaries. For his life see R.A. Nicholson, *A Literary History of the Arabs*, Cambridge University Press, 1969, pp. 292–95.

6　In the third century after Hijra (ninth century AD) a large number of books of anecdotes (*nawader*) as well as a number of monographs on individual humorists were written. However, none were preserved in their original form. Ibn Nadim in his great bibliography *al-Fihrist* mentions a number of relevant authors, among them Abu'l-'Ayna. Franz Rosenthal in his *Humor in Early Islam* (University of Pennsylvania Press, 1956, p. 12) gives his name as "Mohammad b. al-Qasim (807– 896)" and says that Abu'l-Ayna's anecdotes also are found in *Iqd al-Farid* and *al-Aghani*, and they are widely represented in Arab literature.

7　Abi Harith. He seems to be one of the early Arab humorists like Abu'l-Ayna.

20

A man who claimed to be a prophet was brought to Caliph Mu'tasim[8]. The caliph said, "I truly believe that you are a stupid prophet." He answered, "That is true, because I have been sent to people like you."

21

A man stole a robe and took it to the market to sell. Someone else stole it from him. He was asked, "How much did you sell it for?" He said, "For the same price that I bought it."

22

A man claimed to be God. The ruler of the time ordered him to be imprisoned. Someone saw him in prison and asked him, "Can God be in prison?" He answered, "God can be anywhere."

23

In a race a horse was leading the rest. A spectator was boasting and beside himself with joy. Another man asked him, "Is this your horse?" "No," he said, "but his bridle is mine."

24

A man with bad breath went to see a physician, complaining of a toothache. When he opened his mouth, a terrible smell came out. The physician said, "This is not a job for me. You need a different cleaning service."

25

A man said to Hajjaj,[9] "Last night I saw you in a dream, and it seemed that you were in heaven." Hajjaj replied, "If your dream is true, then the injustice in the world to come is even greater than it is here."

---

8 Caliph Mu'tasim, Abu Ishaq al-Mu'tasim was the eighth Abbasid caliph who ruled from 833 until his death in 842 A.D.

9 Hajjaj b. Yusef (d. 714) was the tyrannical viceroy of Caliph Abdu'l-Malik in Iraq. Hajjaj ruled over Iraq and his cruelty and stern disciplinarian measures became proverbial.

26

They said to a Sufi, "Sell your special cloak." He said, "If a fisherman sells his net, with what shall he fish?"

27

A Bedouin went on pilgrimage and arrived at Mecca before the others. He took hold of the curtains of the Ka'ba and said, "O God, forgive me before the crowd gets to you."

28

A fool is a man who comes at the wrong time and stays too long.

29

A man got married, and on the fifth day after the wedding his wife gave birth to a son. The man went to the market and bought writing pads and ink. They asked him, "What are these for?" He answered, "A child that can come into the world after five days will surely go to school in only three more."

30

A drunken old man was brought to Caliph Hisham ibn Abdu'l-Malik[10] with a bottle of wine and a lute. The caliph said, "Break his tambourine on his head and flog him for drinking raisin wine." The old man sat down and began to cry. They said, "Why are you crying? No one has flogged you yet." He replied, "I cry not for being flogged but because you called my lute a tambourine, and worse, he called the musk wine raisin wine." The caliph liked his remarks and let him go.

---

10 Hisham b. Abdu'l-Malik. After Abdu'l-Malik ibn Marwan he was succeeded by his four sons, the last being Hisham (724–743), who was a wise and able ruler.

PERSIAN ANECDOTES

1

Sultan Mahmud,[1] accompanied by Talhak,[2] the jester, attended the sermon of a certain preacher. When they arrived the preacher was saying that whoever had made love to a young boy, on the Day of Judgment would be made to carry him across the narrow bridge of *Sirat*, which leads to heaven. Sultan Mahmud was terrified and began to weep. Talhak told him: "O Sultan, do not weep. Be happy that on that day you will not be left on foot either."

2

A man from Hamadan was going into his house when he saw a handsome young man coming out. He was offended and said: "A curse upon this kind of life you lead! Why do you keep going into the houses of other people? Damn it all, get yourself a wife like everybody else, so you can satisfy the needs of ten other men."

3

A man said to an interpreter of dreams: "I dreamed that I was making eggplant casserole from the dung of a camel. What does this mean?" The dream interpreter answered: "Give me two gold coins first, and then I will tell you the meaning of it." The man replied:

---

1 Sultan Mahmud the Ghaznavid reigned from 998 to 1030; his capital was Ghazna.

2 Talhak, as has been mentioned, was the court jester of Mahmud. Some of the early dynasties of Iran, like the Saljuks and Gaznavids, were originally brought to the region as slaves from Central Asia. Cyrus Shamisa, in his book, *Shahedbazi dar Adabiyyat-i-Farsi* (Tehran, 2003), states that the Gaznavids were of Turkish origin, and that homosexuality was prevalent and often forced upon them. As an example of this he gives the love of Sultan Mahmud for Ayaz. Thus, the jester is referring to Sultan Mahmud's childhood and is implying that the latter was abused in his youth as well.

"If I had two gold coins, I could buy the eggplants and not have to dream about making a casserole from camel dung."

4

Caliph Mahdi [3] got separated from his army one day on a hunting trip. At night he came upon the house of a nomadic Arab and ate a humble meal there. The Arab brought out a jug of wine. After they had drunk a cup, Mahdi said: "I am in the retinue of Caliph Mahdi." After the second cup was served, the caliph said: "I am one of the lieutenants of Mahdi." After drinking a third cup, he said: "I am Mahdi himself." The Arab took the jug away, saying: "You drank the first cup and claimed to be a servant; with the second you became an emir; and with the third you claimed to be the caliph himself. If you drink another cup you will certainly claim to be God." The next day, when the army was once again united with Mahdi, the Arab fled in fear. Mahdi had him brought into his presence and rewarded him with some gold. The Arab said: "I swear that you were telling the truth, even if you claimed to be the fourth one!"

5

A certain person arrived at a graveyard and saw a very long grave. He inquired about whose grave it was. They said: "It is the grave of the Prophet Mohammad's flag-bearer." He said: "Have they buried him with his flag?"

6

They sent Talhak on a mission to the court of the Kharazmshah. [4] He remained there for some time, but he did not get the attention he desired from the king. One day, he was telling stories about different birds and their characteristics in the presence of the king. He said, "The stork is the smartest of all of the birds." They asked him:

---

3 Caliph Mahdi (909–934) was the third Abbasid Caliph who engaged in numerous successful wars, among them the war against al-Mukkana', the veiled Prophet of Khorasan. Mahdi's reign was a time of great prosperity, though he was particularly cruel toward freethinkers and heretical sects.

4 Kharazmshah Takesh Alp Arsalan (1172–1200) became a king in 1194, and four years later he brought a large part of Central Asia under his power.

"How do you know?" He said: "Because he never comes to the court of Kharazm."

7

A man claimed to be God. They took him to the caliph, who told him: "Last year, a man was here claiming to be a prophet, and we had him killed." The man said, "You did the right thing, because I had not sent him."

8

Abu Bakr Robabi[5] went stealing one night, but as hard as he tried, he could not get anything. He "stole" his own turban and hid it under his arm. When he came home, his wife asked: "What have you brought?" He said: "I have brought this turban." "But this is your own turban," she said. "Be quiet," he answered, "You don't understand. I have stolen it so that I don't get out of practice in my profession."

9

Juha [6] would steal a sheep, slaughter it and give its meat as alms. He was asked: "Why do you do that?" He said, "Giving alms compensates for the sin of stealing, and I get to keep the intestines and the fat."

10

Talhak had a few donkeys and Sultan Mahmud ordered them to be taken for unpaid labor to see what he would do. He was annoyed and wanted to complain to the sultan. Under instruction from the king he was told that he could not have an audience that day. Talhak

---

5 Abu Bakr-i Robabi, "the rebeck player," was a musician and jester at the court of Mahmud the Ghaznavid. According to one contemporary poet, Farrokhi (d. 1038), he had a wonderful voice. Another poet, Manuchehri of Damghan (11th century) laments the death of many great poets such as Rudaki, Shahid of Balkh, etc., and says, "Now, instead, Abu Bakr-i Robabi and Juha the satirist have a brisk market" (see Ali Akbar Dehkhoda, *Lughatnama* under "Abu Bakr-i Robabi." He is also mentioned in Anecdote No. 17 in the present collection). Also see *Manuchihri Damhgani va-Musiqi* by Husian-Ali Mallah, Tehran, 1985 pp. 104–106.

6 For Juha see page 86.

went around the royal palace and arriving under the window of the room where the king was sitting, shouted, "The cuckold who does not give an audience, why does he need people's donkeys to work for him unpaid?"

11

When Juha was young he became an apprentice to a tailor for a few days. One day his master brought a bowl of honey to the shop. He wanted to leave the store for an errand, so he told Juha: "There is poison in this bowl. Don't eat it or you'll die." Juha answered, "I will have nothing to do with it." As soon as his master was gone Juha exchanged a piece of cloth for a large loaf of bread and ate all of the honey with it. His master returned and asked for the piece of cloth. Juha told him, "Promise not to beat me, and I will tell the truth. It happened that I was careless and a thief stole the cloth. I was afraid that you would come and beat me. So I decided to eat the poison so that when you returned I would be dead. I ate all of the poison that was in the bowl, and I am still alive. Now you can do whatever you want to me."

12

Juha's father gave him two fish to sell. He went around the streets until he came to the house of a very beautiful woman. She said, "Give me one fish and I will make love with you." Juha gave her the fish and received what she had offered in exchange. Having enjoyed it tremendously, he gave her the other fish and made love to her a second time. Then he sat by the door of the house and said, "I would like to have a drink of water." The woman gave him a pitcher of water; he drank it and then threw the pitcher to the ground and broke it. Juha suddenly saw the lady's husband coming, and began to cry. The husband asked him, "Why are you crying?" Juha said, "I was thirsty and asked for some water at this house. The pitcher slipped from my hands, fell, and broke. I had two fish and now this fine lady has taken them in exchange for the pitcher. Now I dare not return home for the fear of my father." The man reproached his wife saying, "So what if he broke the pitcher?" Then he took the fish and gave them to Juha, so he could go home happily.

13

They once asked a notorious freeloader if he had an appetite. He said, "Poor me. It is the only thing that I have in the whole world."

14

A man from Qazvin went to fight the heretics[7] carrying a large shield. A big stone from the fortress hit him on the head, hurting him badly. He was annoyed and said, "You fools! Are you blind? Why did you hit me on the head? What do you think this huge shield is for?"

15

The son of a Qazvini fell into a well. The father said, "Oh, my dear, don't go anywhere until I go and get a rope to pull you out."

16

A muezzin would call out and then run. He was asked, "Why are you running?" He said, "They say that my voice is beautiful from afar. I was running so that I could hear it from a distance."

17

A thief went to the house of Abu Bakr Robabi. He was awake and ensconced himself in front of the door, leaving the thief no way out. Then Abu Bakr called, "Oh, Shadi" (which was the name of his slave girl). The thief was forced to answer. Abu Bakr said, "Come and rub my feet." The thief rubbed his feet and Abu Bakr got an erection. He said, "Oh, Shadi, come here and let us make love." The poor man had to give in and Abu Bakr made love to him once. After a while Abu Bakr said, "Oh, Shadi, come here and let us repeat it." So he slept with the thief three or four times. The thin horse of a neighbor was tied in the garden, and Abu Bakr told the thief, "Oh

---

7 The heretics were the Isma'ilis (Assassins or Hashshishins) who followed Hasan Sabbah (d. 1124) and terrorized many parts of Iran and Syria. They were known as the followers of the "Old Man of the Mountain" in the West. Their last fortress was destroyed by Hulagu in 1257.

Shadi, go and water the horse." The thief went to the well. The bucket had a hole and as much as he tried he could not pull enough water to quench the horse's thirst. Finally, after troubling the man by every possible means, Abu Bakr pretended that he was asleep. The thief seized the opportunity and ran away. He saw some other thieves who were tunneling under the wall of the same house. He said, "O friends, don't waste your time. In this house there is nothing of value, except for a homosexual who has taken an aphrodisiac and never tires of screwing, and a horse who has been affected by dropsy that no amount of water can satisfy."

18

A man from Ardabil told a physician that he was sick. The doctor took his pulse and said, "To regain your health, every day you must eat five fat well-roasted chickens and saffroned lamb stew[8] with honey and throw it up immediately." The patient said, "What a wise man you are! If somebody else should eat such food and throw it up, I would be the first to eat it."

19

In Kashan a preacher was saying that on the day of Resurrection the custody of the holy well of *Kothar*[9] will be with Imam Ali (the cousin of the Prophet), and that he will give its water to the man of anal integrity. A man from the audience got up and said, "Your reverence, if this is the case, he will have to put it back in the pitcher and drink it all himself."

20

Muwlana Azud al-Din[10] had an assistant called Ala al-Din, who accompanied him on a trip. On the way they stopped, and Ala al-

---

8 In the original, *motanjah* and *agilieh*. The former is apparently a very elaborate dish prepared of lamb and the latter is used for various meat dishes. See *Ashpazi Dawreh-yi Safavi*, edited by Iraj Afshar, Tehran, 1981, pp. 162–65, and 201.

9 *Kothar* is a heavenly well in paradise.

10 Azud al-Din Iji (d. 1335), who is mentioned earlier, was a great scholar and philosopher. Hafez in one of his poems cites him as one of the five great men who made the province of Fars famous during the reign of Sheikh Abu Ishaq Inju (1341–1357).

Din drank some wine. Muwlana called him several times, and after a while he came running and was drunk. Muwlana realized that he was drunk and said, "Ala al-Din, I thought you were with me on this trip, but now I see that you are not even with yourself."

21

There was a governor of Khorasan called Khalaf.[11] Once he was told that there was a certain man who looked much like him. He called the man and asked him, "Was your mother a saleswoman frequenting the houses of the nobility?" The man answered, "My mother was a shy woman who would not go out of the house, but my father worked as a gardener in the houses of the great men."

22

A number of Qazvinis had gone to fight the (Isma'ili) heretics. On their return each man was carrying a head on his spear. One man was carrying a foot. He was asked, "Who killed him?" He answered, "I did." "Then why didn't you bring his head," they asked. He answered, "Before I arrived and killed him, they had already taken away his head."

23

Someone asked his holiness Azud al-Din, "How is it that in the time of the caliphs people would often claim to be God or a prophet but now they don't?" Azud al-Din answered, "These days people are so oppressed by tyranny and hunger that they can think neither of God nor of prophets."

24

A man told his friend, "My eyes hurt. What should I do?" His friend said, "Last year my tooth ached, so I pulled it out."

---

11 Apparently, Khalaf is a reference to the last king of the Saffarids, Khalaf Ibn Ahmad. He succeeded his father in 974 in Sistan and parts of Khorasan and later was defeated and captured by Mahmud. He died in Mahmud's prison in 1021. Khalaf was a patron of many well-known poets.

25

A bald man went to a public bath, and, as he was leaving, he found his hat stolen. In answer to his outcry the bath-keeper said, "When you came here you had no hat." "My good man," the man replied, "Is this the kind of head that you can take out without a hat?"

26

A Qazvini put his right foot into the stirrup and mounted the horse, but he was facing the back of the animal. When told that he had mounted the horse backwards, he said, "It is not me, but the horse that is backwards."

27

A woman and her son fell into the hands of a Turk[12] in the wilderness. He raped them both and left. The woman asked her son, "If you see him again, would you recognize him?" He answered, "His face was towards you. You should recognize him better."

28

One day Sultan Mahmud was very angry, and Talhak wanted to change his mood. He asked, "O Sultan, what was your father's name?" The Sultan was annoyed and turned away from him. Talhak walked around him and once more asked the question. The Sultan said, "Cuckold! What do you want my father's name for?" Talhak retorted, "Now we know what your father's name was. What about your grandfather's name?" Thus the sultan was made to laugh.

29

Three friends from Ray, Gilan and Qazvin went to Mecca for pilgrimage. The Qazvini was poor, but the other two were wealthy. When the man from Ray took hold of the sacred ring of the *Ka'ba*, he said, "O God, in gratitude for bringing me here I free my slave girls Bilban and Banafsheh. When the Gilani took the ring, he said, "O God, thanking you for this pilgrimage, I free my slave boys

---

12 Obeyd sometimes uses Turk and Mongol interchangeably. See, for instance, the second chapter of his "Definitions".

Mobarak and Sonqor." The Qazvini took the ring and said, "O God, you know that I have neither Bilban and Banafsheh nor Mobarak and Sonqor. I express my gratitude by freeing the mother of Fatima by a three-fold divorce."[13]

30

A woman went to Caliph Watheq[14] and claimed to be a prophetess. He asked her if Mohammad was a prophet. She said, "Yes." "But he has said that there will be no prophet after him," the caliph argued. The woman said, "But he has not said there will be no prophetess after him."

31

A carpenter took a wife, and after three months she gave birth to a son. The father was asked, "What shall we call this boy?" He said, "Since it took him three instead of nine months to come to this world, he must be called the royal courier."

32

They brought an eggplant dish to Sultan Mahmud when he was very hungry. It pleased him greatly and he said, "Eggplant is a tasty dish." A court favorite who was present gave a lecture in praise of the eggplant. When the sultan was full, he declared, "Eggplant is a very harmful thing." Then the same courtier made an exaggerated speech on the harmfulness of the eggplant. The sultan asked in amazement, "You wretch! How come you are not praising it anymore?" The man said, "I am your courtier, not that of the eggplant. What I say has to please you, not the eggplant."

---

13 See "threefold divorce" above. "The mother of Fatima" refers his wife. It was considered impolite to mention a married woman's name, so she was called "the mother of such-and-such child."

14 Caliph Watheq (842–846) was the ninth caliph of the Abbasids. This is the same caliph about whose strange life the English author William Beckford wrote his Gothic novel, Vatheq.

33

Mas'ud the astrologer saw Majd al-Din Homayounshah[15] working in his garden. He asked, "What are you planting?" "Nothing very useful," was the reply. The other retorted, "Your father was the same. He too never sowed a useful seed."

34

There was a Turk who would go to public baths and after coming out would claim that his clothes had been stolen. He became such a nuisance that no bath-keeper would allow him in. One day he went to a bath and took several witnesses that he would not make a scene and that whatever claim he makes would be a lie. When he went in, the bath-keeper took all of his clothes and sent them to his own house. The Turk came out and could not make any claims. He came out naked and fastened his quiver and scabbard on his naked body and said, "O Musulmans, I would not make any claims, but you ask the bath-keeper if I had come here dressed like this."

35

Atabek Sulghurshah[16] gave Majd al-Din[17] a shirt made of Egyptian cotton on which was written, "There is no God but Allah." It was worn out, and Majd al-Din did not like it. Someone in the room asked, "How is it that the writing is not followed by 'Muhammad is His Prophet?'" He replied, "This was made before Muhammad was made a prophet."[18]

---

15 This man seems to be a local emir.

16 Atabek Salghur Shah was one of the kings of the Salghurid dynasty that ruled Fars and some parts of Iran from the late twelfth to mid-thirteenth century. This person must be Atabek Sa'd Ibn Abu Bakr who was one of the patrons of the poet Hamgar.

17 Maj al-Din Hamgar (d. 1279) was a native of Yazd and a protégé of Baha al-Din Juwayni, the high-handed governor of Fars, who died in 1279. For the life of this poet, see E. G. Browne, *A Literary History of Persia*, III, pp. 119–24.

18 The formula of the confession of Islam is: "There is no God but Allah, and Mohammad is His Prophet."

36

Sheikh Sharaf al-Din Daragazini[19] asked Muwlana Azud al-Din, "Where has God mentioned the clergy in the Qur'an?" "Next to the learned," he answered, "where He says, 'Are the learned and the ignorant equals?'"[20]

37

A certain person claimed to be a prophet, so they took him before the Caliph Ma'mun.[21] The caliph said, "This is caused by hunger, which has unsettled his brain." He called his cook and said, "Take this man to the kitchen. Give him good food and scented drinks and make him a fine bed until his brain is rested." The man stayed in the kitchen for some time in luxury. His brain was rested. One day, Ma'mun remembered him, and asked for him. He asked, "Does Gabriel still appear before you?" The man said, "Yes, and he told me, 'A wonderful chance has fallen into your hands. Such an easy life has never been granted even to a prophet. Take care not to leave this place.'"

38

A Qazvini[22] had lost his donkey and was going around the town saying that he was grateful. He was asked why he was so grateful. He said, "If I had been riding the donkey I would have been lost for the past four days."

39

Juha came to a certain village and was hungry. He heard a funeral dirge from a house so he went in and said, "Give alms and I will make this man come to life." The dead man's relatives served him

---

19 Sheikh Sharaf al-Din Daragazini was a Sufi of the Qalandariya order.

20 Qur'an, 39: 29.

21 Ma'mun was the seventh caliph of the Abbasids (814–833) and the son of Harun al-Rashid. He became caliph in 813 after having his brother Amin put to death. This story is versified by Jalal al-Din Rumi (1207–1273) in *Mathnavi* (Book V).

22 Qazvinis are associated with numerous humorous stories. Obeyd, being a native of that city, apparently feels free to attribute every funny incident to his fellow citizens. Sharaf al-Din Damghani was apparently a well known scholar.

food and treated him well. When he was full, he said, "Take me to the deceased." Seeing the man he asked, "What was his profession?" They said that he was a weaver. He bit his finger in anguish and said, "Alas! If he had been anything else I could have brought him back, but the weavers, when they die, they really die."

40

A Christian converted to Islam and was taken around town in a procession. Another Christian saw him and said, "Were there not enough Moslems that you became converted, too?"

41

The fortunate vizier Rashid al-Din[23] was suffering from foot pain. One day he was being carried to the court of the king in a palanquin by two handsome young Turkish slaves. Shams al-Din Muzzafar saw him and recited this verse, "This is what remains of the clan of Moses and Aaron being carried by angels."

42

The door of Juha's house was stolen. He went to a mosque and took its door home. They asked him why he did such a thing. Juha said, "My door has been stolen. The owner of this door knows the thief. If He shows me the thief I will give back His door."

---

23 Rashid al-Din Fazlullah (1247–1318) was the famous minister of Ghazan Khan, Ultaitu and Abu Said and one of the great historians of Iran. He began his career as the physician of Abaqa Khan, and later became the prime minister for three of his successors. He devoted his time and wealth to the establishment of schools, libraries, hospitals, and the planning of new cities. His famous work *Jawama' al-Rashidi* (Collected Chronicles) on the history of the Mongols, is based on their own documents, and the general history of the Hebrews, Ancient Iranians, Muslims, Turks, Chinese, Indians and Franks. In writing this "world history" he sought the help of some Italian, Indian, and Chinese travelers and scholars who were at the court of Ghazan. Rashid al-Din was accused of being of Jewish origin and here Obeyd is insinuating the point. Eventually, he fell out of favor and was killed. His rival was the minister Khajah Ali Shah, who built the famous citadel or Arg of Tabriz, and it was through his intrigues that Abu Sa'id ordered Rashid al-Din to be cut in half at the age of 73.

41

A woman had a lover called Mohammad, who was a tailor. One day her husband was consulting her, saying, "Tomorrow I want to bring some friends home. Name anyone who could make a good addition." The woman said, "Also bring Mohammad the tailor." He invited him too. When they had eaten dinner, they got up from the banquet. Mohammad went inside and amused himself with the lady of the house. The husband found out and went into the room. He tried to catch him, but he only could get hold of his penis. Being wet, it slipped out of his hand and Mohammad got away. The husband chased him all the way to his house but could not catch him. When he got back, his wife was indignant and would not speak to him. He said, "Dear lady, what sin have I committed that you hold me in disfavor? I brought Mohammad the tailor as you commanded me. I fed him. You made love to him. I cleaned his penis and accompanied him all the way until he reached the safety of his own home. If there has been any shortcoming on my part, please point it out so that I can apologize for it. And if there is any other service that I can render, tell me and I will rise to the occasion."

42

As Muwlana Sharaf al-Din of Damghan[24] was passing the door of a mosque, he heard the mosque attendant beating a dog that had wandered inside. The dog was barking loudly. Muwlana opened the door and the dog got away. He reproached the attendant, saying, "O friend, please excuse the dog, for he doesn't know any better. He entered the mosque because he lacks intelligence. We who have intelligence, do you ever see any of us inside?"

43

A beggar came to the door of a house asking for a piece of bread. A young girl was home and she told him, "There is nothing here." He asked for some firewood. She said, "There isn't any." "A bit of salt," he asked. "There isn't any," she replied. "A pitcher of water." "None." "Where is your mother," he asked. The girl replied that she

---

24 Sharaf al-Din of Damghan was a well known scholar.

had gone to a relative's funeral. The beggar said, "From what I have seen of the state of your house, ten other relatives should come and mourn for you."

44

A man from Shiraz was cooking bhang in a mosque. The attendant saw him and rebuked him severely. The Shirazi looked up and saw a lame, bald and half-blind man. He said, "You fool, God has not favored you all that much that you should now defend His house so vehemently."

45

An Arab went to Mecca on pilgrimage and his turban was stolen. He said, "O God, once in my life I came to Your house and You had my turban stolen. If You ever see me here again have my teeth broken."

46

A woman had very beautiful eyes. One day, she brought a charge against her husband before a judge. The judge was licentious and was attracted to her eyes. Desire overwhelmed him, and so he took her side. The husband understood what was going on and pulled her veil off her head. The judge saw her face and found it rather unattractive. He said, "Get up, woman. You may have the eyes of the oppressed but you have the face of the oppressor."

47

A policeman came across a drunk Qazvini one night. He told him, "Get up so I can take you to the jail." The man said, "If I were able to make my way, I would rather go to my own house."

48

A man made ablutions in the public bath. The bath attendant asked for money. Having none, he passed wind and said, "Now, I owe you nothing."

49

A Khorasani was carrying a ladder in order to pick fruits from a garden. The owner of the garden arrived and said, "What are you doing in my garden?" He said, "I am selling this ladder." "In my garden," the man asked. The Khorasani replied, "This is my ladder and I can sell it wherever I want."

50

A certain Qazvini had a hatchet and every night he would put it in a safe place and secure the door. His wife asked him, "Why do you put the hatchet in the closet?" He answered, "So that the cat won't get to it." She asked, "What would the cat do with a hatchet?" He said, "You are a foolish woman. He took six pieces of meat that were not worth ten cents. Do you think I am going to leave a hatchet lying around that I paid six coins for?"

51

Muwlana Qotb al-Din[25] visited a prominent man. He asked him, "How are you feeling?" The man said, "I had a fever and my neck was bothering me. But fortunately, one or two days ago my fever broke; however, my neck still hurts." Muwlana said, "Be of good cheer and let us hope that in a few days that will break too."

52

A certain Khorasani went to a doctor and said, "My wife is sick. What should I do?" The physician said, "Tomorrow, bring me a urine specimen in a bottle so that I can look at it and tell you what the cause is." By chance, the Khorasani also became sick that day. The next day, he brought the urine specimen to the doctor. A string was tied around the middle of the specimen. The doctor asked, "Why have you tied this string?" He said, "I became sick too. The upper half is my urine and the lower half is that of my wife." The next day, the doctor related this story at every assembly. A Qazvini

---

25 Muwlana Qotb al-Din of Shiraz (1250–1310) was a famous scientist and physician who wrote numerous works on scientific and philosophical subjects. For his life see, Z. Safa, *Tarikh-i-Adabiyat-i-Iran*, Tehran, 1973, Vol. II, part III, pp. 1227 *et seq.*

was present and said, "Pardon this lack of intelligence on the part of the Khorasanis. Tell me, was the string tied to the inside of the specimen bottle or the outside?"

53

A man told his friend, "I had fifty pounds of wheat. Before I knew it, the mice had eaten it all." His friend said, "I had fifty pounds of wheat also, but before the mice knew it, I had eaten it all."

54

A man asked a preacher what is the name of Satan's wife. He said, "Come here, I will tell you." The man went to him and the preacher said in his ear, "You pimp! How would I know?" When he returned to his place, he was asked what the answer was. He said, "Whoever wants to know should go ask his holiness himself."

55

An Isfahani peasant went to the house of Khajeh Baha al-Din Sahib Divan[26] and told his chamberlain, "Tell your master that the Lord is outside waiting to see him." Khajeh summoned him and asked, "Are you the Lord?" The man replied, "Yes." Khajeh asked, "How?" The peasant replied, "Formerly I was the Lord of the village, the garden, and the house. But your agents have forcibly taken the village, the garden, and the house, so now I am only the Lord."

56

A Khorasani lost his donkey in a caravan. He took another one and put his goods on it. The owner of the donkey caught him and said, "This is mine." He denied it. They asked him, "Was your donkey

---

26 Baha al-Din Sahib Divan was the son of the famous vizier of Abaqa Khan
(1265–1282), Shams al-Din Mohammad the Sahib-Divan. Baha al-Din died in 1279
and was one of the few members of the family to die a natural death. He was one of
the tyrants of his day, and Browne writes: "He was a terribly stern governor (of Persian
Iraq), who inspired the utmost terror in the hearts of his subjects, and whose ferocity
went so far that he caused his little son, and he a favorite child, to be put to death
by his executioner because in play he had caught hold of his beard (*A Literary History
of Persia*, III, p. 21), Baha al-Din's father was put to death by Arghun (1284–1291) in
1284 along with his seven sons and two brothers.

male or female?" He said, "Male." They said, "This one is a female." He said, "Well, my donkey was not much of a male."

57

Someone saw a thief in his garden with a sack tied full of onions. He said, "What are you doing in this garden?" The thief replied, "I was just going my way and suddenly a wind cast me into the garden." He asked, "Why did you dig up those onions?" The thief replied, "When the wind seized me I grabbed these onions by the roots and pulled them out of the ground." The man said, "I can accept that, but who gathered them and tied them in that sack?" He said, "By God, I was just thinking about that when you came."

58

A Qazvini lost a ring in his house. He was searching for it in the street because it was too dark in the house.

59

Someone wanted to say his prayers in the house of a Qazvini, and asked him, "Which way is the *qibleh*?"[27] The Qazvini replied, "I have been in this house only two years. How do I know which way is the *qibleh*?"

60

An Arab was saying his prayers behind an Imam, who, after reciting the first chapter (of the Qur'an[28]), quoted, "The Arabs are the ones most hardened in disbelief and hypocrisy." The Arab was annoyed and gave the man a hard slap on the neck. In the second part of the prayer the Imam recited, "And of the Arab there is he who believeth in God and the Day of Judgement." The Arab said, "You crook! The slap changed your mind."

---

27 The *qibleh* is the direction of Mecca to which every Moslem turns his or her face five times a day in prayer.

28 The first chapter of the Qur'an (al-Fatihah) has only seven verses and should be recited twice at each of the five times of prayer. After this another chapter is elective, but normally a very short chapter is chosen. Here the preacher quotes a different verse in order to appease the Arab.

61

A poet saw a man making love to a boy in a mosque. He made a big fuss and rebuked him for committing sodomy in the house of the Lord. The man kept watching the poet, and one day saw him doing the same thing in the mosque. He said, "What was that you were telling me, and now you are doing it yourself?" The poet answered, "Have you never heard of poetic license?"

62

The governor of Nishapur said to Shams al-Din, the physician, "I cannot digest food. What do you advise me to do?" He replied, "Eat what has already been digested."

63

A woman was present at the meeting of a certain preacher. When she came home, she told her husband, "The preacher said that they will build a house in heaven for whoever has intercourse with his lawful wife tonight." That night when they went to bed, the wife said, "Get up if you desire a house in heaven." The man made love to his wife once. After some time passed, she said, "You have built one house for yourself. Now build another one for me." So he built another one. After a while she said, "What shall we do if we have company?" So the man built a guest house as well. The next day, the man caught his wife unaware and had anal intercourse with her, saying, "Anyone who has built three houses in heaven should build at least one in hell."

64

A certain Qazvini had a toothache so he went to a surgeon. The surgeon said, "Give me two coins and I will pull it out." The Qazvini said, "I won't pay more than one coin." When the pain became unbearable, he was compelled to pay two coins. He brought his face close and showed him a tooth that was not bothering him. The surgeon pulled it. The Qazvini said, "I made a mistake." Then he showed him the tooth that was really aching, and the surgeon pulled it out. The Qazvini said, "You wanted to take advantage of me and take two coins, but I am more clever than you. I made a fool of you and got my own way so that I got two teeth pulled out for the price of one."

65

A man got married. On the wedding night, when he and his wife were left alone, the man went out to do something. When he came back to the room, he saw the bride piercing her ears with a needle. When they made love he found out that she was not a virgin. He got angry and said, "Lady, the holes which you should have bored in your father's house, you are doing here, and the one you should do here, has already been done in your father's house."

66

A certain man claimed to be a prophet. They brought him before the caliph. He asked him, "What is your miracle?" The man said, "My miracle is that I can read whatever is in your heart. What is now in the hearts of all is the belief that I am lying."

67

A great man had a beautiful wife named Zohreh. He had to go on a journey, so he had a white dress made for her and gave his servant a bowl of indigo dye and said, "Whenever the lady of the house commits an indecent act, put one finger of dye on her dress, so that when I return, if you are not here, the state of things will be clear to me." After a while, the master wrote to the servant:

> *Has Zohreh done anything which is a disgrace,*
> *To have on her dress any indigo trace?*

The servant replied:

> *If in the master's return there be further delay,*
> *A leopard will become your beloved Zohreh!*

68

A Qazvini on his death bed passed wind. Someone asked, "Are you not ashamed before the people present?" He said, "When am I going to see them again, so that I should be ashamed before them?"

69

A man from Shiraz was making love to his wife. She had not removed her pubic hair, as was the custom, and it was too long. He got annoyed and said, "This is all right with me since I am your husband and intimate with you, but you should really be ashamed if a stranger finds you like this."

70

A man from Luristan was present at the congregation of a preacher. The preacher was saying, "The bridge of *Sirat* (which leads to heaven) is narrower than a strand of hair and sharper than the blade of a sword, and on the Day of Judgment everyone must pass over it." The man asked, "Is there a rail or something to hold on to?" The preacher said, "No." The Lur said, "You are making a fool of yourself, sir. Not even a bird can pass over it."

71

A certain judge had colic. The doctor told his family to give him a wine enema. They poured a lot of wine into him, and the man got drunk. He started beating his family and yelling. They asked his son, "What is your father doing?" He said, "He is making a riot from his bottom."

72

They asked a preacher, "What is Islam?" He replied, "I am a preacher. What should I know about Islam?"

73

A Turkman had a lawsuit. He filled a vat with plaster and covering it with butter gave it to the judge. The judge took the side of the Turkman, and passing the verdict in his favor gave him a sealed letter as he had desired. After a week the case was discovered, and the judge called him and said, "Bring back the letter. There is an error in it, which should be corrected." The Turkman replied, "There is no error in the letter. If there is any it must be in the vat."

74

A Qazvini came back from Baghdad in the summer. They asked him, "What were you doing there?" He said, "Sweating."

75

A poor dervish was saying his prayers with his shoes on. A thief who had his eyes on the shoes said, "It is not right to pray with your shoes on." The dervish, who knew the intention of the man, replied, "If my prayers are not accepted, at least I will have my shoes."

76

A Qazvini went on a lion hunt. He was roaring and breaking wind. They asked him, "Why are you roaring?" He said, "So that the lion will be afraid." "Why are you farting," they asked. He said, "Because I am afraid, too."

77

One night a thief broke into the house of a poor man. The man woke up and said, "My dear fellow, what are you searching for in the dark that we look for in daylight and don't find?"

78

A Qazvini was going to battle without any arrows. He was saying that the arrows will come from the enemy. Someone said, "Perhaps they will not come." He replied, "Then there won't be a battle."

79

A witty man saw some fried chicken on the table of a miser. It had been served for three days in a row, and still it was not completely eaten. He said, "This chicken has lived longer in death than it did in life."

80

Talhak said, "I had a dream that was half true and half false." "What was it," they asked. He replied, "I dreamed that I was carrying a treasure on my shoulders. It was so heavy that I wet myself. When

I got up I found out that my bed was wet but there was no trace of the treasure."

81

The wife of Talhak gave birth to a child. Sultan Mahmud asked him what it was. He replied, "What else is born to poor people? Either a boy or a girl." The sultan said, "Then what is born to great men?" Talhak said, "Something that swears at people and destroys their lives."

82

Talhak was asked, "What is cuckoldry?" He replied, "This you have to ask of judges."

83

Talhak's mule was stolen. Someone said, "It is your own fault since you did not watch it." Another man said, "The groom is to blame for leaving the stable door open." Talhak said, "Then, in this case, the thief is not to be blamed at all."

84

A man who was hard of hearing said to a Qazvini, "I heard you have gotten married." The Qazvini said, "By God! You don't hear anything. How did you hear this?"

85

A man made his guest sleep on the lower floor of his house, but in the middle of the night he heard him laughing upstairs. He said, "What are you doing there?" The guest said, "I rolled up in my sleep." He replied, "But people roll down, not up." The guest said, "That is exactly why I am laughing."

86

A tailor was making a cloak for a Turk. The Turk was so watchful that the tailor could not steal a piece of the material while cutting it. Suddenly the tailor farted, and the Turk laughed and laughed until he fell on his back and the tailor managed to accomplish what he wanted to do. Then the Turk got up and said, "Master tailor, do that again." The tailor replied, "No, I shouldn't, because then the cloak will become too tight."

87

They gave a Qazvini a job as a night watchman in a certain town. One afternoon he arrested a man and said, "I am the night watchman and I must take you to jail." The man said, "A night watchman does not arrest people during the day." The Qazvini said, "Where will I find you tonight?" People gathered around and prevented the Qazvini from taking the man. He said, "All right, I'll let you go now, but you must promise to return tonight."

88

A certain Khorasani had a very thin horse. They asked him, "Why don't you give this horse some barley?" He said, "He is allocated ten pounds of barley every night." "Why then is he so thin," they asked. "Because," he replied, "I owe him one month's worth."

89

Majd al-Din Hamgar[29] had a very ugly wife who was away on a trip. One day he was in a meeting when his slave came running, "Oh, master, my lady has descended on the house." Majd Hamgar said, "If only the house had descended on your lady."

---

29 See note 17 of this chapter. According to *Tarikh-i-Gozideh,* when the poet came from Yazd to Isfahan, he left his elderly wife behind, but she soon followed him. News of her arrival was brought to the poet by one of his pupils. He said, "Good news! Your lady has alighted in the house." "Good news," replied Majd al-Din, "would rather be that the house would alight on her!" The lady to whom this was reported reproached her husband for his unkind words, quoting the quatrain of Omar Khayyam beginning: "Before you, or even I, have existed the days and the nights." "Before me, perhaps," replied Majd al-Din, "but heaven forbid that day and night should have existed before you!" (E. G.Browne, *A Literary History of Persia,* III, p.119)

90

Sultan Mahmud was lying down with his head on the knee of Tal-hak. Suddenly he asked, "What is your relation to cuckolds?" Talhak replied, "I am their pillow."

91

Shams al-Din Muzaffar[30] was saying to his students, "One should learn in childhood, because whatever you learn in childhood you never forget. For instance, I learned the first chapter of the Qur'an when I was a child, and now after fifty years, though I have never repeated it, I still remember it."[31]

92

A certain person shot an arrow at a bird and missed. His friend shouted, "Bravo!" The archer was annoyed and said, "You are making fun of me." The friend said, "No. I was saying 'Bravo' to the bird."

93

Someone had stolen Talhak's shoes when he was in a mosque and thrown them into a church. He said in amazement, "It is strange that I am a Moslem and my shoes are Christians."

94

A preacher said from his pulpit, "Whenever a man dies drunk, he is buried drunk, and he will rise drunk from his grave." A man from Khorasan who was at the foot of the pulpit said, "By God! One bottle of such a wine is worth a hundred gold coins!"

95

Muwlana Qotb al-Din was making love to someone in his room in the school. Suddenly someone put his hand on the door of the room and opened it. Muwlana said, "What do you want?" He said, "I want somewhere to sit down and say my prayers." Muwlana

---

30 Shams al-Din Muzaffar. I could not find a reference for this man.

31 As was said in note 27, the first chapter of Qur'an should be recited in prayers at least ten times a day by every Moslem.

replied, "Are you blind? Don't you see that this place is so small that people have to pile on top of each other?"

96

One night, in the presence of Sultan Abu Saʻid[32], there was a Sufi dance. The king took Muwlana Azud al-Din[33] by the hand and commanded him to dance. While his reverence was dancing, someone said, "Oh, Muwlana, you are not dancing according to the rules." "I don't dance by the rules," he replied. "I dance by decree."

97

For the feast of Nowruz[34] Sultan Mahmud gave everyone a robe of honor, but he ordered a donkey saddle to be given to his jester Talhak. Talhak came into the presence of the Sultan with the saddle on his back, and, turning to the dignitaries, said, "Gentlemen, see how gracious the king has been to me. He has given each of you robes of honor from the treasury, but he has given me the robe off his own back!"[35]

98

A certain person had eaten some yogurt, and a little of it had spilled on his beard. Someone asked him, "What have you been eating?" He answered, "A young pigeon." The other said, "You must be telling the truth since its droppings can still be seen on your beard."

99

During a famine Juha arrived at a village and heard that the headman was ill. It happened that when went he to his house they were baking bread. He said, "He could be cured if you bring me some bread with butter and honey." So they did. Juha kept putting the

32 Sultan Saʻid (1317–1334) was the last king of the Ilkhanid dynasty upon whose death the line of successors of Hulagu came to an end.

33 Azud al-Din Iji was a great scholar and philosopher and a contemporary of Obeyd. See note 10 of this chapter.

34 Nowruz is the festival of the New Year among Iranians and falls around March 20th on the spring equinox.

35 This story was made into a play during the reign of Naser al-Din Shah (1851–1896).

butter and honey inside the bread, turning each morsel around the head of the sick man, and then putting it into his own mouth until everything was finished. Finally he said, "Today's treatment is enough. I will be back tomorrow." Shortly thereafter the head-man died. They asked Juha, "What kind of treatment was this?" He replied, "Don't question it! If I had not eaten the bread, I would have died before him."

100

A man brought a sheikh home as his guest and put some cushions behind him. Behind the cushions there were some gold coins, and the sheikh stole them. The man searched for the gold coins and found them missing. The sheikh said, "Tell me whoever you suspect from those present so that we can search them." The host said, "Sheikh, I suspect those present but I am sure of you."

101

Harun asked Bohlul[36], "Who is the most dear to you?" He replied, "The one who feeds me well." Harun said, "I will feed you well. Then you will be my friend." Bohlul said, "You cannot have friendship on credit."

102

A woman had survived two husbands and her third husband was deathly ill. She was crying and asking him, "Oh, my dear, where are you going and who do you entrust me to?" He replied, "To the fourth cuckold."

103

A woman asked Talhak, "Where is the candy shop?" He said, "Inside the lady's skirt."

---

36 Harun al-Rashid (786–809), who was mentioned earlier in these notes, is the famous fifth caliph of the Abbasid dynasty. Bohlul was his contemporary and a kind of "sagacious fool," who would dispense wisdom while pretending to be a fool. They say Harun wanted to appoint him to be the judge of Baghdad, but in order to avoid this post Bohlul pretended to be insane.

104

Abu Bakr Robabi [37] took the harpist Khar Maghzi [38] home as his guest. It was a cold winter night and the latter could not sleep because of the cold. He said, "Master Abu Bakr! Please throw something on my bed." He put a piece of an old rush mat that was in the house on him. After a while Khar Maghzi asked for something more. He brought a ladder and put it on the bed. After a while the guest asked for something warm. The day before the neighbors had washed their laundry and there was a tub with some water still in it, and Abu Bakr put it on top of the ladder. Khar Maghzi moved and the water spilled and went through the rush mat and he cried out, "Oh, Master Abu Bakr! Be kind enough to remove the top blanket, for now I am sweating."

105

A preacher was giving a sermon and among the audience was a man who was crying mournfully. The preacher said, "Learn sincerity from this man who is really touched and is weeping." The man got up and said, "Sir, I don't know what you are talking about, but I had a goat with a red beard just like yours, who died two days ago. Whenever you talk and move your beard I remember that goat and cannot stop crying."

106

A preacher on the pulpit was saying, "Writing the names of Adam and Eve and hanging them in the house will keep Satan away." Talhak got up and said, "Sir, while they were living next to God in heaven, Satan seduced them. How do you expect their names to keep him away from our houses?"

107

Satan was asked, "Which class of people do you like most?" He said, "Salesmen." They asked the reason. He said, "I was content with lies from them, but they added false oaths as well."

---

37 For Abu Bakr Robabi see note 5.

38 *Khar Maghzi* literally means "someone with a donkey's brains."

108

A coffin was being carried to the grave and a poor man was standing on the road with his son. The son asked, "Father, what's in there?" His father replied, "A person." The son asked him again, "Where are they taking him?" The man said, "To a place where there is no food, no clothes, no wood, no fire, no gold, no silver, not a mat or a rug." The son said, "Surely, father, they are taking him to our house."[39]

109

The father of Juha had a slave-girl with whom he occasionally would have intercourse. One night Juha crept into her bed and embraced her. She asked, "Who are you?" He said, "Me, my father."

110

There was a madman in Baghdad named Ibrahim. One day he was a guest in the house of the vizier of the caliph, but he could not get anything to eat except some loaves of barley bread. After a while they said that a three-karat sapphire was missing, and so they stripped and searched everyone present but did not find the jewel.

---

39 This story also is given by Rumi in his *Mathnavi* (R. Nicholson's translation, Book II, pp. 383–4):

> A child was crying bitterly and beating his head beside his father's coffin,
> Saying, "Why, father, where are they taking you to press you tight under
> some earth?
> They are taking you to a narrow and noisome house: there is no carpet in it,
> nor any mat;
> No lamp at night and no bread by day; neither smell nor sign of food is there.
> No door in good repair, no way to the roof; not one neighbor to be (your) refuge.
> Your body, which was a place for the people's kisses how should it go into a blind
> and murky house?
> A pitiless house and narrow room, where neither (your) face will be lasting nor
> (your) color."
> In this manner was he enumerating the qualities of the house whilst he wrung tears
> of blood from his two eyes.
> The father said to Juhi, "Don't be a fool!" "O Papa," said he, "Hear the marks
> (of identity).
> These marks which be mentioned one by one our house has them (all), without
> uncertainty of doubt
> (It has) neither mat nor lamp nor food; neither its door is in good repair, nor its court
> nor its roof."

Believing that someone had swallowed it, they decided to keep Ibrahim and some others in the house for three days, so that the gem might come out from one of them. After three days Ibrahim saw the caliph and shouted: "O caliph! I have eaten only a loaf of barley bread in this house and have been confined here, for the last three days, with you saying that I have stolen a three-karat sapphire. You who have much luxury and have wasted so much wealth, what will be done to you?"[40]

---

40 This story is attributed to Bohlul by Farid al-Din Attar (1136–1234) in his *Mosibat-nameh* (ed. Nurani Vesal, p. 117):

> One day the drunken Bohlul
> Climbed the throne of Harun.
> The royal guards beat him such
> That blood from his every wound did gush.
> Being soundly beaten, he moaned:
> "Oh, Harun, king of the world!
> I sat for a while upon this throne,
> And behold me thus inflicted with wounds;
> You who for a lifetime occupied the same
> Joint by joint will they separate your frame
> For sitting here one moment so dearly I have paid;
> What will be forthcoming for you instead?

CAT & MOUSE

TRANSLATED BY DICK DAVIS

NOTES BY HASAN JAVADI

Come, listen to my tale. If you're discerning,
Possessed of wisdom, common sense or learning,
I guarantee that it'll knock you flat –
This story's of a mouse, and of a cat.

O wise and knowledgeable one, rehearse
This Cat and Mouse tale in well-ordered verse,
Like pearls that roll from rhyme to chiming rhyme.
In old Kerman[1] then, once upon a time,
There lived a lion-tailed cat – huge, dragon-jawed,[2]
Pot-bellied, barrel-chested, leopard-clawed.
He'd miaow – and roaring lions would leave their feast
Fleeing in terror from the savage beast.
He dropped by at his favorite bar one day
To hunt for mice – and waiting for his prey
(Just like a thief behind a rock) our cat
Prepared his ambush, prone behind a vat.

Then suddenly a little mouse peered out,
Saw the coast clear and gave his squeaky shout,

---

1 There is a manuscript of Obeyd's works in the Majlis Library of Tehran, dated 1540, in which some lines of "Mush u Gorba" are different from the published versions of it. In the following notes the most significant differences are noted. For example, here the Majlis MS. has: "I heard a blood-thirsty cat lived in Kerman."

2 There are two extra couplets in the Majlis MS.: *With the bride he would go to bed / When he was a guest in the house of the groom / He would overlook the pot, bowl and ladle / And he would supervise the house and the table.*

Dashed for the vat and let his mouse head sink
Deep in the dark intoxicating drink.
Now roaring drunk he cried, "Where is that cat?
I'll cut his head off and I'll flay the brat,
I'll stuff his skin with straw; that cat to me's
The most contemptible of enemies".
The cat sat listening and he hardly breathed;
Slowly his teeth were bared, his claws unsheathed,
And then he pounced and like a leopard pinned
The mouse who squirmed and squealed, "I know I've sinned,
I'm sorry, I…" The cat replied, "I heard –
You hypocrite, you Moslem[3] – every word,
You can't fool me". And there and then he killed
The mouse and ate it. With his belly filled
He strolled off to the mosque, and glibly said
His prayers as if a mullah born and bred:[4]
"Court of the Highest, I repent; no more
Will my sharp teeth be soaked in mouse's gore –
And for the blood that I've unjustly shed
I'll give the poor as alms twelve pounds of bread".
He prayed and moaned and heaved such bitter sighs
That tears stood brimming in his feline eyes.
Behind the pulpit lurked a little mouse
Who quickly bore the news off to his house:
"Great news, the cat's converted, he repents,
He's filled with sacred Moslem sentiments;
This paragon of pious virtues keeps
Prayer vigils in the mosque, and moans and weeps".

Then when they heard the news the laughing mice
Seemed blessed with all the joys of paradise,

---

3 In the original in Turkish and in an obscene manner, the cat says :
   "O Musulman, I will ravish your wife!" This is another indication that the mice were
   Turkish-speaking Moslems.

4 The original phrase is in Arabic: "Verily God has made this our portion."

And seven elders of the mousey nation
Were chosen as a special deputation –
Each of them carried something rare and fine
To give the cat: one bore a glass of wine
And one a spit of lamb-kebab, another
Took currants in a salver, while his brother
Sported a tray of figs, one cheese he'd made,
And one a syrup of sweet lemonade,
One bore him yogurt, butter and fresh bread,
The last a tray of rice upon his head.
The mice drew near the cat – and with salaams
And deepest bows and eulogistic psalms
They greeted him: "O thou, for whom all mice
Would undergo the final sacrifice,
Accept the gifts we offer you, o lord."

　　　He peered at them, and chanted "Your reward
Will be in heaven; I've fasted now for days
To please the Merciful beyond all praise;
Whoever does God's work it's certain he
Will be rewarded, and abundantly!"
Then he continued: "But come closer, do…
Dear friends, a few steps more, a very few…"
Then, frail as trembling aspen leaves, the mice
Went forward as a group – and in a trice
The cat leapt like a mighty champion, like
A fighter[5] who sees when and where to strike;
Five mice he captured – two in each front paw
And one was snapped up in his lion-like jaw.

　　　The two remaining mice that got away
Fled crying "Slothful mice, o rue the day –

With claws and teeth the cat's dismembered five
Of us and only we remain alive".

5　"Like a warrior". Interestingly enough Obeyd uses the word *mubarez* for a "warrior,"
which might be a reference to Mubarez al-Din Mohammad.

Then at this bitter news the grieving crowd
Donned mourning clothes, lamented long and loud,
Heaped dust upon their heads, and contrite cried,
"Alas for our great leaders who have died!"
At last the mice were able to agree,
"We'll tell the king of this calamity;
Before the throne we'll chronicle our case –
The foul oppression of the feline race".

The mouse king sat upon his throne in state;
Far off he saw his subjects congregate
Until they came before him as a crowd
And, with a single motion, deeply bowed:
"O king of kings and of the ages king
This cat has done a hideous, dreadful thing,
O king of kings, we are your sacrifice,[6]
An annual one of us would once suffice
To feed this cat; but, since his late conversion,
Since he's become a pious Moslem Persian,
Five at a time is now his greedy style".
And when they'd whimpered and complained a while
The king replied: "My dearest subjects, wait!
        I'll be revenged upon this reprobate,
I'll kill this cat in such a way the story
Will fill the world with my eternal glory".
He spent a whole week mustering his men,
Three hundred thousand mice-at-arms, and then
Another thirty thousand; each mouse bore
A bow and spear and shield, and longed for war;

Now like a wave they poured in from Gilan,
From distant Rasht and fertile Khorasan.[7]

---

6 While the mice address the king, they say in Turkish : "May we be your sacrifice." This
   again is an indication that the king of mice spoke Turkish.

7 Khorasan and Gilan. These names indicate that the king's domain included eastern

The brave victorious mouse addressed the horde,
"I speak now as your leader and your lord,
A mouse must be our envoy to this cat;
Our message is, 'Submit, or failing that
You must prepare yourself for endless war'.
There was an ancient mouse-ambassador[8]
Who was entrusted with the valiant plan;
He traveled to the cat's lair in Kerman
And there he bowed and said, "I represent
The noble mouse-king and his government,
And bear a message meant for you alone:
You must pay homage to the mouse-king's throne;
War is the price if you do not submit!"
The cat replied, "I never heard such shit!
I'll not budge from Kerman!" But secretly
He summoned cats to his confederacy,
Cats like lions, cats from Isfahan,
Wild cats from Yazd, cats from his own Kerman;
And when their army'd grown they set out for
The destined conflict, well-prepared for war.
       Across the desert marched the mousey horde,
Down from the hills the feline army poured,
The plain of Fars became their battlefield –
Each side fought bravely and refused to yield.
(So great the slaughter was no man could say
How many cats and mice were killed that day.)
       The cat sprang like a lion, and attacked
The center where the mice were thickly packed –
But one mouse trailed his horse, the cat spun round[9]
And as he spun fell headlong to the ground;

and northern Iran respectively, while the Cat's realm, as shown by Isfahan, Yazd, and
Kerman, was central and southeastern Persia.

8 The Persian text says: "From old there was an ambassador, a vizier of the army…"
This could be a reference to Khajeh Emad al-Din, the minister of Shah Abu Ishaq, who
served as a messenger between the two kings.

9 This might be a reference to Mubarez al-Din's horse being hamstrung
(see introduction).

"Allah is with us" cried the mice, "we've won,
Grab him, grab the cats' doughty champion!"
They beat their war-drums wildly to proclaim
That victory was theirs, and martial fame,
The troops milled round, excited, jubilant,
Mobbing their mouse-king on his elephant.
The cat's front paws were tied and tightly bound,
They forced him as a suppliant to the ground,
The king's command rang out, "String up that cat,
Hang the abominable black-faced brat".

But hearing this, his feline pride provoked,
The cat seethed like a cauldron, panted, choked…
Then like a lion he knelt and gnawed to shreds
His captors' bonds; they snapped like flimsy threads.
He grabbed the nearest mice and glared around
Then flung them with contempt against the ground –
The mice fled squeaking in a mass defection,
Their king fled in the opposite direction:
The elephant, his royal rider too,
His wealth and crown and splendid retinue,
Decamped and disappeared; on that wide plain
Not one of them was ever seen again.

And all that's left is this peculiar story
Bestowing posthumous, poetic glory
On old Obayd-e Zakani.
                    My son
Consider carefully who lost, who won:
Store up this story's useful implications,
Remember it in tricky situations.

BIBLIOGRAPHY

PERSIAN SOURCES

Ahmad, Amin. *Razi Haft Iqlim*, Calcutta, 1929 (under Qazvin).

Asemi, Mohammad. "Muwlana Nezam al-Din Obeyd-e Zakani," in *Payam-i Nuvin*, vol. 1, no. 9, pp. 1–15.

Dastghaib, A., "Hezl-i Obeyd-e Zakani," in *Payam-i Nuvin*, vol. 5, no.2, pp. 42–59.

Davudi, Nasrallah. *Dar Shenakht-e Obeyd-e Zakani*, Mashhad, 1966.

Obeyd-e Zakani, *Akhlaq al-Ashraf*, edited with annotations by Ali Asghar Halabi, Tehran, Asatir, 1995.

———. *Resaleh-ye Delgosha, Nawadir, Ta'rifat, Sad Pand ve Navadir-i Amthal*, edited and annotated by Ali Asghar Halabi, Tehran, Asatir, 2004.

Javadi, Hasan, "Tanz dar dastan-Heyvanat," Alefba, Tehran, 1977, pp. 1–22

Javanmard, A. "Yek Monaqed-i Bozurg-i Ijtimai'," *Paik-i Solh*, no.1, pp. 37–46 and 57–65.

Khanlari, Parviz Natel, "Yek Monteged-i Ijtema`i Zabardast, Obeyd-e Zakani," *Sokhan*, vol. 3, pp. 408–12 and 525–30.

Khayyampour, P., *Farhang Sokhanvaran*, Tabriz, 1960, p. 383.

Mostofi, Hamd Allah, *Tarikh-e Gozidah*, ed. Abdul Husain Nawa'i, Tehran, 1957, pp. 804–30.

Pour-Javadi, Nasrullah, *Negahi Digar, "Az Qazvin beh San Francisco,"* Tehran: Rouzbehan, 1988.

Ruk al-Din Humayun, Farrokh, *Hafez-e Kharabati*, Tehran, 1974, vol. 1, pp. 404–34; vol. 3, pp. 1664–94 and 2328–33.

Samarqandi, Dawlatshah, *Tazkirat al-Shu'ara*, ed. Mohammad Abbasi, Tehran, 1958, pp. 322–28.

Shamisa, Sirus, *Shahidbazi dar Adabiyyat-i Farsi*, Tehran: Ferdaus Publications, 2003.

Vamiqi, Iraj, "Obeyd-e Zakani Latifa-saray-i Qarn-i Sukut", *Nigin*, vol. 1, nos. 5–7.

Varasta, Khosrow, "Obeyd-e Zakani, Hazzal ya Hakkim", *Mardomshenasi*, vol.1, pp.128–37; 179–88; and vol.2, pp. 175–82.

Yusefi, Gholam-Husain. *Didari be Ahl-i Qalam*, Mashhad: Ferdausi University Publications, 1976, pp. 287–312.

Zabih, Allah Safa, *Tarikh-e Adabiyat dar Iran*, Tehran, 1973, III, 2nd Part, pp. 963–85.

EDITIONS OF OBEYD'S WORKS IN PERSIAN

Daruish, Parviz, illustrator. *Mush u Gorba-ye Obeyd-e Zakani*, Tehran, 1976.

Farnud, Gholam-Hussain, ed. *Hajviyat va Hazliyat-e Obeyd-e Zakani*, Tehran, 1968.

Ferté, H., ed. *Lata'if-e Obeyd-e Zakani*, with an introduction by Mirza Habib, Isfahani, Istanbul, 1303/1885–6. The same edition was reprinted in Tehran in 1954.

Halabi, Ali Asghar. *Akhlaq al-Ashraf*, edited with annotations, Tehran, Asatir, 1995.

———. *Obeyd-e Zakani*, Tarh-i Now Publications, Tehran, 1998.

Iqbal, Abbas, ed. *Kulliyat-e Obeyd-e Zakani*, Tehran, 1963. This edition was reprinted several times, the latest being by Parviz Atabaki with some additions in1957.

Mahjub, Mohammed Ja'far, ed. *Kulliyat-e Obeyd-e Zakani*, Persian Text Series, New York: Bibliotheca Persia Press, 1999. (This is the most up-to-date and accurate text of the collected works of Obeyd, carefully edited and annotated by the late Professor Mahjub.)

———. *Obeyd-e Zakani, Bagh-i Delgosha* (selections). Dushanbeh: Nashiryat-i Erfan, 1969.

Qishmi, Muhsin, ed. *Javidaneh Obeyd-e Zakani* (Selections). Tehran: Salis, 2001.

Sprachman, Paul. "Fal-nameh-i Buruj," *Ayandeh*, 5, nos. 10–12 (Winter 1979): 738–49.

Usha, S.A., ed. *Divan-e Obeyd-e Zakani* (without the satirical works). University of Madras, 1952.

SOURCES IN EUROPEAN LANGUAGES:

Arberry, A. J. *Classical Persian Literature*, London, 1958, pp. 288–300.

Aryanpur Kashani, Abbas. *The Story of the Cat and Mice*, rendered into English verse, Tehran, College of Translation, 1971.

Bajraktarevic, F. "Zakaniijeve definiciije," *Stvaranje* (Cetinje), 11 (1956): 500–504.

Bausani, Alessandro. *Storia della Letteratura Persiana*, Milano, 1960, pp. 450–63.

———. "Il 'Libro della Barba' di Obeid Zakani," A Francesco Gabrieli (Universita di Roma, *Studi orientali publicati a cura della Sculla orientale*, vol. 5), Roma: 1964, pp.1–19.

Browne, E. G. *A History of Persian Literature under Tartar Dominion*, Cambridge University Press, 1920, pp. 230–59

Bunting, Basil, "The Pious Cat" in *Uncollected Poems,* ed. Richard Caddel, Oxford University Press, 1991.

Christensen, Arthur. "Les Sots dans la tradition populaire des Persans," *Acta Orientala*, 1–3, 1923–24, pp.43–47.

———. "Remarques sur les faceties de 'Ubaid-e-Zakani, avec des extraits de la Risala-i-dilgusa," *Acta Orientala*, III, 1925, pp.1–37.

———. "En persisk Satiriker fra Mongolertiden," *Studier fra Sprogog Oltidsforskning*, no. 131, Kopenhagen, 1924.

D'Erme, Giovanni M. *Opere Satiriche di 'Ubayd Zakani* in *Iranica a cura di Gherardo Gnoli e Adriano* V. Rossi, Napoli: Instituto Universitario Orientale, Seminario Studi Asiatici, Series Minor, 1979.

Farzad, Masud. *Rats against Cats*, London, Priory Press, 1945; reprint edition with text and illustrations of Mahmood Javadipoor, Tehran, 1963.

Javadi, Hasan, *Satire in Persian Literature,* Fairleigh Dickinson University Press, 1988.

Kondireva, N. "Obeid Zakani: Veselaya kniga," *Per. predisli Prim. N. Kodirevoi. Stikhi per G. Alekseevim,* M., "Nauka," 1965, p.178.

Pound, Omar. 'Ubayd Zakani, *Gorby and the Rats*, London, Agenda Editions, 1972.

Sprachman, Paul, *Suppressed Persian: An Anthology of Forbidden Literature,* Mazda Publishers, Costa Mesa, CA, 1995.

Surieu, Robert, *Sarv-e Naz: An Essay on Love and the Representation of Erotic Themes in Ancient Iran,* English translation by James Hogarth, Geneva, Nagel Publishers, 1967.

INDEX

OBEYD-E
ZAKANI

Printed in the United States
123873LV00009B/88-105/A

9 781933 823225